Interactive Readings for
Christian Worship

Interactive Readings for Christian Worship

Melvin Campbell
and
Edwin Zackrison

iUniverse, Inc.
New York Lincoln Shanghai

Interactive Readings for Christian Worship

iUniverse, Inc.

For information address:
iUniverse, Inc.
2021 Pine Lake Road, Suite 100
Lincoln, NE 68512
www.iuniverse.com

ISBN: 0-595-29227-5

Printed in the United States of America

Contents

A Word of Introduction to Worship Leaders

UNRESPONSIVE RESPONSIVE READINGS

Think about it for a moment. Isn't a "responsive reading" supposed to be *responsive?* But, honestly, aren't most of the responses you hear from your congregations what you might call "less than exciting." Are they not too often slow, in low voices and tedious—like a large, cumbersome sound, the voices rather than *responding in the gladness and joy of worship?* In congregational singing you hear excitement, harmonies, soprano voices, deep bass parts resonating. In responsive readings too often everything is in dull, lifeless monotones.

Part of the problem simply centers in what we expect of an audience in terms of spontaneity. Would God object if we rehearsed the audience and introduced them to exciting reading that corresponds to the excitement of their experience with Christ?

Responsive readings are not new to most churches or worship leaders. For most of us they have been a part of our Christian worship heritage for as long as we can remember. In that regard this book is not *new.* But we think you will find these responsive readings *fresh.*

READING WITH A DRAMATIC FLAIR

We have drawn from four common dramatic forms in composing these scripts: traditional responsive form, readers theatre, traditional drama and choral reading. Those familiar with these forms will recognize some of the techniques for maintaining interest, attention, and involvement.

Both of us have experienced lifeless responsive readings in church worship. We were sure something could be done to improve our own involvement. With that in mind we began writing what you have here. We decided that worship leaders may encourage their audiences all they wish but they need the help of a well-written script as well.

Traditionally Christian scripts for responsive readings have simply called for repeating verses of scripture arranged alternately for reader and audience. It has apparently mattered little how long these passages are. But in congregational reading unless there is *some* rehearsing with the group (which virtually never happens) the longer the passage the less spontaneous the response becomes.

READING WITH A PURPOSE

These responsive readings differ from the traditional approach. Here you may find the audience cast in various roles (such as in drama) where they will respond as a character in a story (such as in readers theatre). Good reading is easy to achieve (as in choral reading) and the audience gets to answer and suggest corporately (as in traditional responsive readings).

The audience may play the fool, the pharisee, the publican, God, the believer, or the skeptic. At all times we worked at keeping the responses short so that the long monotony of untrained reading would be avoided, and a minimum of rehearsal instruction would be needed.

FROM NEW YORK TO AUSTRALIA

All the readings in this book have been field-tested, sometimes in many different congregational settings. We have written them, tried them, rewritten them, tried them again, and in some cases rewritten them yet again. From New York to Australia and many points in between we traveled together or by ourselves and tested these readings. We have sent them to churches of various denominations and received helpful critical reviews and suggestions from worship leaders and pastors. We think they will work well with virtually any size congregation.

We originally wrote and tested each one on a group of about 200. But we have used them in small churches and big churches as large as 3000 with encouraging results. Other testing settings have included college classrooms, Church Schools, vesper programs and chapel programs.

We invite you to enjoy the uniqueness. We see a destination in discovering responsive readings that live and contribute to the body life we enjoy and need. As a new community in Christ we believe in the freshness of life. Let our worship show it!

The didactic aspect of worship used to be taken for granted. In most churches, certainly in Protestant churches, people assumed that when they went to church they did something with their mind—they thought, they contemplated, they considered, they reasoned, and the like.

FRESH APPROACH TO AN OLD FORM

Today in Protestant worship, and to some degree in Catholic as well, moves are being made to include those feelings and emotions that indicate involvement of the whole being in worship to God. Whether we like it or not the charismatic movement has had its impact on our worship. As a result the old approach to responsive readings doesn't cut it with fresh, exciting, worship styles of today's generation.

We have sought to meet this need with a fresh approach to an old form. We call these "interactive readings" because they sort of dare the congregation not to be involved. Our hypothesis has been that if people can be cast as players in the responsive reading rather than just required to plod through long lines of reading matter, the old didactic aspect of worship may stand a chance and people may learn and enjoy while they are worshiping.

A few years ago many of us were moved by the "I'm Okay, You're Okay" movement, also called Transactional Analysis. The writers in this form of psychological approach to communication reminded us that we all have certain "hungers." These include the hunger to be affirmed, accepted, and stroked. We also have a hunger to lead and to regulate other people's time. And we have a hunger to have our time structured. Worship should meet all of these hungers. But of equal value to all these hungers is the last one which this approach calls "excitement hunger." That means we all have the need to have our time structured excitingly.

COME WORSHIP GOD

None of us wants to participate in meaninglessness. The church in all ages sought meaning. But when meaningful forms were adopted as religious or Christian traditions the danger of them losing their meaning became a real possibility. For this reason we believe that we need continually to be injecting old forms with freshness. If we are afraid of entertaining people we might make a serious mistake to the other side. We may well forget that we all have a basic, felt need to have time structured excitingly.

We challenge all worship leaders to take advantage of our humble efforts to meet this need which we believe all Christians have! Enjoy the worship of God. Make it appealing to the young! We submit these readings in anticipation that this will be your experience.

Melvin Campbell, Riverside, California
Edwin Zackrison, Ringgold, Georgia

1

A Hymn to the Fool

Scriptural Base: Psalms 14, 53; Proverbs 10–30; Ecclesiastes 4–7
Subject: Wisdom, God's Description of Foolishness

Background of the Selection

The wisdom writers of the Old Testament had a great deal to say about those who denied the existence of God. Their favorite description was "fool." Only the fool says "There is no God." As a result of this presupposition, the fool's thinking follows a certain pattern. Psalms, Proverbs, and Ecclesiastes, in particular, spell out this pattern. This reading underscores the irrationality of the fool—the illogic of the fool's arguments from the divine point of view. In this reading the congregation becomes a chorus of fools so as to feel the inadequacy of playing the fool.

Ideas for Reading

Participants: READER 1, READER 2, and AUDIENCE.

Some lines in this reading stress the illogic of the fool, "It is wise to serve your-self because…it is wise." Other lines emphasize narcissism, "I want **what** I want **when** I want it." Rehearse this briefly with your AUDIENCE either before the wor-ship service or just before the reading. Point out that italicized words should be emphasized. Practice this line too (paying close attention to emphasized words) reading it with a staccato cadence: "**THERE** is no God. There **IS** no God. There is **NO** God. There is no **GOD**." As the text says, the fools are repeating their folly.

A Hymn to the Fool

READER 1: Fools say in their hearts,
AUDIENCE: There is no God.
READER 1: They are corrupt.
READER 2: Their ways are vile.
AUDIENCE: There is no God.
READER 1: A fool does no good.
READER 2: A fool is vile.
READER 1: Fools say in their hearts,
AUDIENCE: There is no God.

READER 1: God looks down from heaven on humankind
READER 2: to see if there are any who understand.
AUDIENCE: There is no God!
READER 1: God looks down from heaven on humankind
READER 2: to see if there are any who seek God.
AUDIENCE: There is no God.
READER 1: Whoever spreads slander is a fool.
READER 2: Whoever brings trouble on the family is not wise.
READER 1: Whoever trusts in self is a fool.
READER 2: A fool finds pleasure in evil conduct.
AUDIENCE: There is no *sin!*

READER 1: People of understanding delight in wisdom.
READER 2: Fools show their annoyance at once.
AUDIENCE: Don't tell me what to do.
READER 1: Reasonable people heed correction.
READER 2: Fools spurn their parents' discipline
AUDIENCE: I want what I want when I want it.
READER 1: Wise people accept commands.
READER 2: Fools give full vent to their anger—
AUDIENCE: You're crazy!
READER 1: A fool is hotheaded and reckless.
READER 2: From the mouth of the fool gushes folly.
READER 1: Wise people keep themselves under control.
READER 2: Fools fold their hands and ruin themselves.

READER 1: Like a lame person's legs that hang limp

READER 2: is a proverb in the mouth of a fool.

AUDIENCE: **There is no devil because there is no God.**

READER 1: Like a thorn bush in a drunkard's hand

READER 2: is a proverb in the mouth of a fool.

AUDIENCE: **It is wise to serve yourself because…it is wise!**

READER 1: Like archers who wound at random,

READER 2: are those who hire a fool.

AUDIENCE: **I don't really care from whom I rob.**

READER 1: Like a partridge that hatches eggs it did not lay,

READER 2: is the fool who gains riches by unjust means.

READER 1: When life is half gone

READER 2: "friends" desert the fool.

AUDIENCE: **Now I *KNOW* there is no God.**

READER 1: A fool multiplies words—

READER 2: No one knows what is coming.

AUDIENCE: **What really matters is what I think.**

READER 1: Like a dog returning to its vomit

READER 2: fools repeat their folly:

AUDIENCE: **"*THERE* is no God. There *IS* no God. There is *NO* God. There is no *GOD*."**

READER 1: Every wise person stores up knowledge.

AUDIENCE: **You don't need God to think.**

READER 2: Every prudent person acts out of knowledge.

AUDIENCE: **You don't need God to live.**

READER 1: Every intelligent person fears the Lord and shuns evil.

AUDIENCE: **You don't need God to succeed.**

READER 2: Every perceptive mind commends knowledge.

AUDIENCE: **You don't need God to learn.**

READER 1: Every discerning heart seeks knowledge.

AUDIENCE: **You don't need God to tell you what's important. There IS no God.**

READER 1: Fools are thought wise if they keep silent

READER 2: And discerning if they hold their tongue—

AUDIENCE: **(silence)**

READER 1: *(pause)* Better to meet a bear robbed of her cubs
READER 2: than fools in their folly.
READER 1: Of what use is money in the hand of fools
READER 2: since they have no wisdom?
READER 1: Do not speak to fools,
READER 2: for they will scorn the wisdom of your words.
READER 1: Wisdom is too high for fools;
READER 2: they have nothing worthwhile to say.
READER 1: Do not answer fools according to their folly,
READER 2: or you will be like them yourself.
READER 1: If you have played the fool
READER 2: and exalted yourself
READER 1: or if you have planned evil
READER 2: clap your hand over your mouth!
READER 1: The fear of the Lord is the beginning of wisdom.
READER 2: Knowledge of the Holy One is understanding.

2

The Unmerciful Servant

Scriptural base: Matthew 18:23–35
Subject: Forgiveness, God's Faithfulness to Humankind

Background of the Selection

Jesus often taught about forgiveness. Perhaps the most succinct teaching of Christ on the subject is from the Lord's Prayer: "Forgive us our debts as we also have forgiven our debtors" (Matthew 6:12, RSV). Jesus' parable recorded in Matthew 18:23–35, gives believers a clearer understanding of the distinction between God's activity and our responsibility in forgiveness. Christ often used money, debts, and paying off those bills as illustrations of the transaction involved in the forgiveness process. Without God's forgiving attitude none of us could look for life. This attitude led to Christ's ethical expectations of his followers even to forgive their enemies (Matthew 5:43–48, cf. Romans 5:8). God's forgiveness, through Christ's atoning work at the Cross, rooted in his grace, is the message of the Gospel. Our forgiveness of others demonstrates how much God's forgiveness has changed us!

Ideas for Reading

Participants: READER 1, READER 2, THE KING, POOR SERVANT, and AUDIENCE.

THE KING and POOR SERVANT are critical to this reading. They should be people who can feel the anger, forgiveness, and frustration of the moment and be able to express it with their voices. They should be placed in the middle of the platform with the READERS at opposite sides of the platform. Well-placed pauses will add to the excitement and hence the interest of the whole presentation. The

5

AUDIENCE must say their lines with feeling. Point out such lines as "Please don't!" and "Pay up!" as lines to be said with passionate feeling. Certainly we become emphatic when we use such lines in real life.

The Unmerciful Servant

READER 1: The kingdom of heaven is like a king
READER 2: who wanted to settle accounts with his servants.
READER 1: A man who owed him several million dollars
READER 2: was brought to him.
THE KING: I need my several million dollars, pay up!
AUDIENCE: I can't pay!
THE KING: Pay up!!
AUDIENCE: I can't pay!
THE KING: Sell his wife!
AUDIENCE: Please don't!
THE KING: Sell him!
AUDIENCE: Please don't!
THE KING: Sell his children! Sell his lands!
AUDIENCE: Please don't!
READER 1: The servant fell on his knees
READER 2: and cried:
AUDIENCE: Be patient, I will pay.
READER 1: And the king took pity on him.
THE KING: Cancel his debt, he is free!
AUDIENCE: I am free, I am free!

READER 1: But when the servant went out
READER 2: he found one of his fellow servants
READER 1: who owed him just a few dollars.
AUDIENCE: Pay up!
POOR SERVANT: I can't pay!
AUDIENCE: Pay up!!
POOR SERVANT: I can't pay!
AUDIENCE: Sell his wife!
POOR SERVANT: Please don't!
AUDIENCE: Sell him!
POOR SERVANT: Please don't!!
AUDIENCE: Sell his children! Sell his lands!
POOR SERVANT: Please don't!!
READER 1: The servant's servant fell on his knees
READER 2: and cried.

POOR SERVANT: Be patient I will pay.
READER 1:But the first servant, ignoring the plea
READER 2: became an unmerciful servant by saying
AUDIENCE: SELL!

READER 1: The king was not pleased at all!
THE KING: I forgave you millions, can't you forgive a few?
READER 1: And so it was in this parable
READER 2: that Jesus gave meaning
READER 1: to what
READER 2: forgiveness really means.

3

The Lost Sheep (Child)

Scriptural Base: Matthew 18:10–14
Subject: Children, God's Faithfulness to Humankind

Background of the Selection

This reading is based on the parable of Jesus in Matthew 18:10–14. The parable illustrates the value of human beings, but in the immediate context the worth of little children. Throughout Jesus' ministry we find him interacting with children and saying things about them that suggest their characteristics are shared in some way with the saved and the kingdom of heaven. The parable of the lost sheep has been consistently overlooked as a parable about the significance of children! So we will underscore this context in this reading.

Ideas for Reading

Participants: READER 1, READER 2, READER 3, READER 4, and AUDIENCE.

Position all four READERS facing the congregation. READERS 1 and 2 should stand together in front on one side of the platform and READERS 3 and 4 should stand together on the other side. The READERS are in a teaching role in this reading. Their lines should be read consistent with the emphasis given by punctuation. For example, ellipsis (…) indicates pause. We will warn you that this reading can sound fragmented if not read right. With a some focus and rehearsing the READERS will be able to make these sentences smooth and discover the delightful effect of several voices cooperating to produce vocal thoughts.

The Lost Sheep (Child)

READER 1: This is a parable
READER 2: about the kingdom of Heaven.
READER 3: The kingdom is
READER 4: is like sheep.
AUDIENCE: Sheep?
READER 3: And a shepherd.
READER 2: And little children who are lost.

READER 4: The kingdom is…
READER 2: is like wandering,
READER 1: losing and looking,
READER 3: finding and laughing,
READER 4: maybe rejoicing!
READER 3: Tell me,
READER 4: what do you think?

READER 2: A man was counting
READER 1: his flock of sheep—
READER 3: One,
READER 1: Two,
READER 2: Three,
AUDIENCE: Four,
READER 3: Seventy-two,
READER 1: Eighty-nine,
READER 2: Ninety-eight,
AUDIENCE: Ninety-nine, one hundred.
READER 3: No,…just ninety-nine!

READER 2: One of them,
READER 1: one of the hundred,
READER 4: wandered off, got lost—
READER 2: hopelessly lost—
READER 4: in the hills—
READER 2: or in the world—
READER 3: which left just
AUDIENCE: ninety-nine.

READER 4: A man owns
READER 1: a flock of sheep—
READER 3: one hundred,
READER 1: to be exact.
READER 4: But now it's
AUDIENCE: ninety-nine—
READER 2: He looks
READER 3: for the one lost sheep.

READER 1: He leaves the
AUDIENCE: ninety-nine
READER 2: on the hills or in the world—
READER 4:...Or wherever—
READER 1: Looks and finds
READER 2: the wandering lost sheep.

READER 3: This is the truth
READER 4: about shepherds and sheep,
ALL READERS: and God and people.
READER 2: When the man
READER 3: finds the sheep
READER 2: he is so happy.

READER 1: Happier about finding the lost—
AUDIENCE: Than keeping the ninety-nine?
READER 4: who didn't get lost
READER 2: or who didn't wander off.

READER 1: This is a parable about little children—
AUDIENCE: Little children?
READER 4: Little children
READER 2: who are lost.
READER 1: and a God in Heaven
READER 3: who is not willing
READER 4: that any little child
READER 2: should be lost.

READER 1: Furthermore—
READER 2: A child—
AUDIENCE: One child?
READER 4: Even just one—
READER 3: is equal to the
READER 4: ninety-nine big people
AUDIENCE: Equal?
READER 2: who were left.
READER 1: For of such,
READER 3: that is, the likes of little children—
READER 4: For of such
ALL READERS: is the kingdom of Heaven.

4

The Secret of Being Content

Scriptural Base: Philippians 1–4
Subject: Confidence in Christ, Faith, Positive Attitude

Background of the Selection

Paul's letter to the believers in Philippi overflows with encouragement, vision, optimism and reality. Anyone facing hardship and worry will especially find direction and comfort here. Writing from prison Paul turns suffering for his faith into strength as he counsels his friends in Christ. Being content in Christ under trial offers courage to us as we see our spiritual life developing realistically.

Ideas for Reading

Participants: READER 1, READER 2, and AUDIENCE.

READERS should pay close attention to the emphases placed in the text by use of italicized words and punctuation. The reading should be very bright and upbeat throughout. The AUDIENCE is cast in the role of responding to the reading of Paul's counsel. Encourage them to read their lines with feeling-usually excitedly.

The Secret of Being Content

READER 1: There are some things
READER 2: of which we in Christ may be confident:
READER 1: He who began a good work in us
READER 2: carries it on to completion.
READER 1: He who produces a love in us
READER 2: make it abound more and more.
READER 1: He who gives us knowledge and depth of insight
READER 2: gives us ability to discern what is best.
READER 1: He who gives us life
READER 2: fills it with the fruit of His righteousness.
READER 1: All of this comes through Jesus Christ alone!
AUDIENCE: Glory and praise be to God!

READER 1: Yet some people preach Christ out of envy.
AUDIENCE: That's sad!
READER 2: Not really!
AUDIENCE: What?
READER 1: And some people preach Christ out of rivalry.
AUDIENCE: That's bad!
READER 2: Are you sure?
AUDIENCE: Of course!
READER 1: But others preach Christ out of goodwill.
AUDIENCE: Yes, that's more like it!
READERS 1, 2: But wait a minute!
AUDIENCE: What do you mean?
READER 1: Does it matter? Think about it!
READER 2: *(pause and think)* No! It really doesn't matter!
AUDIENCE: What?!

READER 1: The *important* thing is
READER 2: that in every way,
READER 1: whether from false motives
READER 2: or from true motives—
READER 1: What really matters is—
READERS 1, 2: That Christ is preached!
AUDIENCE: All right!!

READER 1: So quit your bickering—
READER 2: Quit your arguing—
READERS 1, 2: And just learn to rejoice when Christ is preached!
AUDIENCE: Hallelujah! Amen!

READER 1: You see—
READER 2: Things are not always as they first appear.
READER 1: For example:
READER 2: In prison
READER 1: you may look at things differently.
READER 2: And in trials
READER 1: you may just think of deliverance.
AUDIENCE: *(with feeling)* **0 Lord, make this cup pass from me!**
READER 1: In deep troubles
READER 2: you may consider eternity.
READER 1: In discouragement
READER 2: you may even think of death as a way out.
READER 1: In fact, in tribulation
READER 2: dying can be considered gain.
AUDIENCE: I would prefer to be with the Lord!

READER 1: But for the believer
READER 2: to live, anywhere, is Christ!
READER 1: Continuing to live when you'd rather die
READER 2: is more unselfish.
AUDIENCE: Not my will but thine, O God my Father!
READER 1: For in living—
READER 2: Trials or no trials—
READER 1: Tough times or no tough times—
READER 2: We can encourage others who also suffer.
AUDIENCE: Make us content, O Lord!

READER 1: Learn the secret of being content—
READER 2: Whatever happens, conduct yourselves
READER 1: in a manner worthy of the gospel of Christ.
READER 2: For it has been granted to you on behalf of Christ
READER 1: not only to believe on him,

READER 2: but also to suffer for him.
AUDIENCE: Believing is a privilege.
READER 1: That's right—So is suffering!
AUDIENCE: Suffering is a privilege?
READER 2: Suffering is a privilege!
AUDIENCE: Things are NOT always as they first appear!

READER 1: Be glad and rejoice!
READER 2: Press on toward the goal to win the prize—
AUDIENCE: For which God has called us!
READER 1: Be glad and rejoice!
READER 2: Press on toward the goal to win the prize
AUDIENCE: for which God has called us!
READER 1: The secret of being content
READER 2: is to know that in any and every situation
READER 1: I can do everything
READERS 1, 2: through Him who gives me strength.

5

Our Majestic God

Scriptural Base: Psalm 8, Luke 15
Subject: Worship, God's Greatness, Christian Identity

Background of the Selection

Worship has everything to do with the Object of our adoration. Christians see God as One who deserves worship. Whatever we do and say should bear in mind that this truth makes sense and thus we attempt to build up one's faith in God as a reasonable and worthy Object of worship. Our faith demands that we seek to represent God adequately. The Biblical writers showed God's worthiness of worship by enumerating his accomplishments and actions. Psalm 8 is a meditation on His majesty. It is good for us simply to think about God's kingship and worthiness to rule. This psalm lists some of the reasons why we worship him. The contrasts between God and humankind underscore this majesty. This reading is designed to emphasize those contrasts so that we will be reminded (in our excursions into pride) that God is God and that any rulership we have is because of that fact.

Ideas for Reading

Participants: READER 1, READER 2, READER 3, and AUDIENCE.

READERS 1 & 2 should stand together in front on one side of the platform and READER 3 should stand alone on the other side. The AUDIENCE should say their lines with feeling. Such lines as "Who am I?" and "I am wretched!" should be said with passionate feeling.

Our Majestic God

READER 1: O Lord—
AUDIENCE: *Our* Lord!
READER 2: How majestic is your name in all the earth!
READER 3: Majestic?
READER 1: Excellent!
READER 2: Powerful!
READER 3: Authoritarian?
AUDIENCE: Loving!

READER 2: O Lord—
AUDIENCE: *Our* Lord!
READER 1: Yahweh!
READER 2: Adonai!
READER 1: Savior!
READER 3: Creator?
READERS 1, 2: Creator of all the earth!

READER 1: You have set your glory—
READER 2: Not only in the earth—
READER 1: Not only in the heavens—
AUDIENCE: But in our hearts!
READER 2: Your glory
AUDIENCE: is our hope
ALL READERS: and salvation.

READER 1: From the lips of children and infants,
READER 2: Through their words of weakness,
READER 1: Through their words of innocence,
READER 3: You have ordained praise.

READER 1: Out of the mouth of children
READER 2: comes openness,
READER 3: comes tolerance,
AUDIENCE: comes praise!
READER 1: So a little child shall lead them.

READER 3: When I consider the heavens,
READER 2: the work of your hands—
READER 1: When I think about
AUDIENCE: **things bigger than I—**
READER 1: The moon and stars,
READER 2: the milky way,
READER 1: the unknown that you have set in place—

AUDIENCE: **Who am 1—**
READER 2: that God would think of me?
READER 3: Who am 1—
READER 1: that God should care for me?
READER 2: Who am 1—
READER 1: that I should be crowned with glory and honor?

AUDIENCE: **I am wretched**
READER 2: and naked
READER 3: and blind.
READER 1: Yet I am crowned with glory and honor.
READER 3: God has made us rulers
READER 2: over His created works.
READER 1: Under our feet are the flocks of the hills,
READER 2: herds of the pasture,
READER 3: beasts of the field,
READER 2: birds of the air,
READER 1: fish of the sea.

READER 3: O Lord—
AUDIENCE: ***Our* Lord.**
READER 3: O Lord are we that glory?
READER 2: The lost coins that were found?
READER 1: The pearls that were purchased?
READER 3: The treasure that was uncovered?
READER 1: That you have set us above the heavens?
READER 2: How majestic is your name in all the earth.
READER 3: All of us are
AUDIENCE: **Because God is!**

6

Forgiveness for *Certain* Persons

Scriptural Base: Luke 7:36–50
Subject: Forgiveness, Attitudes, Judgmentalism, Hypocrisy

Background of the Selection

The story of the anointing of Jesus by "the woman of the city, who was a sinner" (Luke 7:37), is one of the greatest demonstrations of love in the Scriptures. Indeed this woman had every reason to demonstrate her love to Jesus for he perhaps was the only man who ever loved her unselfishly and unconditionally. This reading explores the interaction not between Jesus and the woman, but between those men who were condemned by her acts of gratitude. The reading is about outward attitudes and innermost sins.

Ideas for Reading

Participants: READER 1, READER 2, and AUDIENCE.

The READERS will stand in front: they should be separated and use separate microphones if a public address system is available. The READERS could be men or women. One of each would have an excellent effect. Point out to the AUDIENCE and the READERS that the word *"certain"* needs to be read with an irony that bespeaks pharisaical self-righteousness, i.e., *here is one who needs forgiveness but is clearly not worthy of God's attention.*

Forgiveness for *Certain* Persons

READER 1: A Pharisee had invited Jesus
READER 2: to have dinner with him.
READER 1: So—
READER 2: Jesus went, ate,
READER 1: and reclined at the table.
READER 2: While Jesus reclined, a woman—
AUDIENCE: A *certain* woman!
READER 1: Who had led a sinful life in that town,
READER 2: learned that Jesus was eating with the Pharisees.

READER 1: So—
READER 2: She came to the dinner—
AUDIENCE: Uninvited!
READER 2: With tears,
READER 1: with an alabaster box,
READER 2: and with very long hair.
READER 1: The tears wet Jesus' feet,
READER 2: the perfume anointed his feet,
READER 1: the very long hair dried his feet.

AUDIENCE: If Jesus only knew!
READER 2: What kind of woman she was?
READER 1: That she was the city's sinner?
READER 2: That she was a *certain* woman?
AUDIENCE: If he were a prophet he would know!

READER 1: Jesus said, Simon
READER 2: I have something to tell you.
AUDIENCE: Tell me, Master.

READER 1: If two men who owe money,
READER 2: one five hundred dollars,
READER 1: the other five dollars,
READER 2: have their debts cancelled by the banker,
READER 1: which—
READER 2: just which of the two men

READER 1: will love the banker more?
AUDIENCE: The one with the bigger debt.

READER 2: You are correct!
READER 1: Now, do you
READER 2: Now, do you see this certain woman?
AUDIENCE: I can see and smell!
READER 1: I came into your house.
READER 2: Did you give me any water for my feet?
AUDIENCE: I see a *certain* woman!
READER 1: But this woman
READER 2: provided water from her tears.
READER 1: Did you provide me with a towel?
AUDIENCE: I see a *certain* woman!
READER 2: This woman used her hair as a towel.
READER 1: Did you provide me with a towel?
READER 2: Did you give me a gift?
AUDIENCE: No, but she is a—
READER 1: She has used perfume on my feet.
READER 2: Her sins, her many sins, are forgiven
READER 1: so she loves much.

READER 2: Anyone who has been forgiven little
READER 1: loves little!
READER 2: But her many, many sins *are* forgiven!
READER 1: She is a new person.

AUDIENCE: How can sins be forgiven?
READER 1: Her faith has delivered her,
READER 2: she can go in peace.

AUDIENCE: But…what of me?
READER 1: You too can go in peace
READER 2: when you wash and dry my feet
READER 1: and realize that you too are a *certain* person!

7

People Come First

Scriptural Base: Matthew 12:1–14
Subject: Faithfulness, Celebration, Meaning of Obedience

Background of the Selection

The religious leaders of Jesus' day had forgotten the meaning of the Sabbath—a day to celebrate creation and redemption. To them it was an institution to bring the common people under subjection. They used the day with its myriad of rules to condemn and coerce. The most significance aspect of the Sabbath to the Jews was the outward observance with apparently no regard to evil thoughts. Jesus cuts across these petty rules to emphasize that the Sabbath was given for human benefit and that people are more important than rules and animals.

Ideas for Reading

Participants: READER 1, READER 2, and AUDIENCE.

The AUDIENCE plays the Pharisee part until the very end. The reading is trying to convey the idea that many people in Jesus' day never seemed to get the concept that people were more important than rules, regulations, or days. As such the AUDIENCE remains defiant until the end. The READERS are to be placed on either side of the platform. They need to read with cool logic to contrast the irrational thoughts of the Pharisee.

People Come First

READER 1: The Pharisees were watching Jesus

READER 2: even though it was the Sabbath day.

READER 1: Jesus was hungry.

READER 2: Jesus' disciples were hungry.

AUDIENCE: Look!

READER 1: The Pharisees watched the disciples

READER 2: pick some heads of wheat.

AUDIENCE: Sabbath breaking!

READER 1: But Jesus and the disciples continued to pick and eat.

AUDIENCE: Unlawful!

READER 2: To all of this Jesus answered,

READER 1: When David and his companions

READER 2: were hungry, he ate

READER 1: consecrated bread,

READER 2: which was unlawful for him to eat

READER 1: but lawful for the priests to eat.

READER 2: Or did

READER 1: the temple priests

READER 2: desecrate the Sabbath

READER 1: at the temple?

AUDIENCE: But they are innocent!

READER 1: One greater than the temple is here.

AUDIENCE: And who is that?

READER 2: What does it mean

READER 1: when God says,

READER 2: I desire mercy?

AUDIENCE: I don't—

READER 1: What does it mean for God to say,

READER 2: I do not desire sacrifice?

AUDIENCE: I…I don't know—

READER 1: Because you don't know

READER 2: you condemn the innocent!

READER 1: The Lord is—

READER 2: The Lord *is* the Lord of the Sabbath.

READER 1: Here is a man
READER 2: in the synagogue
READER 1: with a shriveled hand—
READER 2: On the Sabbath day.
READER 1: Do you heal him?
AUDIENCE: No, Never!

READER 1: Here is a sheep
READER 2: in a pit,
READER 1: trapped—
READER 2: *On* the Sabbath day.
READER 1: Do you lift it out?
AUDIENCE: Well yes, of course!

READER 2: Are not people
READER 1: of more value than a sheep?
AUDIENCE: Well—
READER 2: Therefore it is lawful
READER 1: to do good *on* the Sabbath day.

READER 2: *On* the Sabbath day
READER 1: the man with a shriveled hand
READER 2: was healed as he held it out.
READER 1: *On* the Sabbath day
READER 2: the Pharisees went out
READER 1: and plotted to kill Jesus.

READER 2: You see the Sabbath—
AUDIENCE: The Sabbath! Thou shalt not!
READER 1: The Sabbath was made for people—
READER 2: People who are hungry—
READER 1: People who need to eat consecrated bread—
READER 2: People who are priests in the temple—
READER 1: And all other people—
AUDIENCE: And especially people who have sheep in pits.

READER 2: And especially
READER 1: for people
READER 2: with shriveled hands and hearts.
READER 1: How much more valuable
READER 2: is a person than a sheep!
READER 1: Remember—
READER 2: That is how you keep
READER 1: the Sabbath day holy.

8

Protection

Scriptural Base: Psalms 23, 91
Subject: God's Presence in Trouble, the Goodness of God, God's Concern

Background of the Selection

Psalms 23 and 91 are best-loved psalms of David. There is a parallel in these two psalms that is seldom noticed. The author had obviously been through frightening experiences and later realized that God was with him in all his troubles. The imagery used in both psalms means a great deal to us in our lives. This reading brings the two chapters together in an effort to reinforce the goodness and greatness of God, his love and concern for each of us.

Ideas for Reading

Participants: READER 1, READER 2, and AUDIENCE.

The AUDIENCE takes the part of God in this reading. The READERS represent the individual who seeks help from God. In this particular reading the AUDIENCE has longer responses than usual. For this reason we suggest two things: first, that you have a third READER taking the lead in the congregation; second, that you practice the longer sentences ahead of time with the AUDIENCE. The Psalmist is writing from his soul. The READERS need to read those thoughts similarly. Position the READERS close together as if they were one person. Do not restrict the reader to any one gender or age group.

Protection

READER 1: The Lord is my Shepherd,
READER 2: I shall lack nothing.
AUDIENCE: I will answer you in trouble.
READER 1: He invites me to lie down in green pastures,
AUDIENCE: Rest in the strength of my almighty arm.
READER 2: He directs me to quiet waters.

AUDIENCE: I am your strength.
READER 1: My soul is restored by him.
AUDIENCE: I am your refuge.
READER 2: He points me to the paths of righteousness,
READER 1: to exalt his Name.
AUDIENCE: My faithfulness will be your shield.

READER 2: Even though I walk—
AUDIENCE: You will tread upon the cobra—
READER 1: through the gorge of the shadow of death—
AUDIENCE: You will be saved from the deadly plague.
READER 2: I have no fear of evil. You are with me.
AUDIENCE: For the terrorism at night, have no fear.
READER 1: Your rod and staff comfort me.
AUDIENCE: Under my wings you will find shelter.

READER 2: You have set a table before me—
AUDIENCE: With long life you will be satisfied.
READER 1: In the presence of my enemies.
AUDIENCE: Ten thousand will fall at your side.
READER 2: You anoint my head with oil;
READER 1: my cup overflows.
AUDIENCE: I will rescue and protect you.
READER 2: Surely goodness and mercy will follow me
READER 1: all the days of my life.
AUDIENCE: I have commanded my angels concerning you—
READER 2: And I will dwell in the house of the Lord—
AUDIENCE: Come, dwell in the Almighty's shelter.
READER 1: Forever?

AUDIENCE: You have seen my salvation—
READER 2: And forever?
AUDIENCE: I am your refuge and strength.
READER 1: Then the Lord is my shepherd
READER 2: 1 shall not want!

9

Sensitivity

Scriptural Base: Selected Old and New Testament Examples
Subject: Obedience, Sensitivity to God's Desires

Background of the Selection

Throughout scripture God is trying to communicate to us his plan for our lives. Over and over he finds people resisting even when they say they do not intend to resist. This reading recounts a few of the times when humankind has ignored God. Although the consequences are not enumerated in the reading they are implied. The fact that God uses a variety of ways to reach us becomes very clear by the end of the reading.

Ideas for Reading

Participants: READER 1, READER 2, and AUDIENCE.

Encourage the congregation to say their lines with feeling. Point out such lines as "He touched it!" and "He cut off an ear!" as lines to be said with expression. Suggest that they think "That's incredible!" while they are saying these lines.

Sensitivity

READER 1: The Lord said to Adam and Eve,
READER 2: Do not eat of the tree of knowledge of good and evil.
AUDIENCE: They ate of it.

READER 1: The Lord said to Cain,
READER 2: Bring a Lamb as the sacrifice.
AUDIENCE: He brought corn.

READER 1: The Lord said to Moses,
READER 2: Speak to the rock and water will come out.
AUDIENCE: He hit it.

READER 1: The Lord said to Nadab and Abihu,
READER 2: Use the fire from the altar.
AUDIENCE: They used *strange* fire.

READER 1: The Lord said to Uzzah,
READER 2: Don't touch the ark.
AUDIENCE: He touched it!

READER 1: The Lord said to Peter,
READER 2: My kingdom is not of this world.
AUDIENCE: He cut off an ear!

READER 1: The Lord said to Ananias and Sapphira,
READER 2: Give.
AUDIENCE: They kept.

READER 1: The Lord said to Saul of Tarsus,
READER 2: Do this.
AUDIENCE: He did *that*.

READER 1: The Lord says to us,
READER 2: Come here.
AUDIENCE: But we go there.

READER 1: The Lord says to us,
READER 2: Listen!
AUDIENCE: But we speak.

READER 1: The Lord says to us,
READER 2: Speak!
AUDIENCE: *(Silence)*

READER 1: *[Count silently 1, 2, 3, 4, 5]* The Lord says to us,
READER 2: Do.
READER 1: But we don't.
READER 2: Give!
READER 1: And we keep.
READER 2: Teach!
READER 1: So we preach.
READER 2: Sense!
READER 1: But we are senseless.
READER 2: Empathize!
READER 1: But we sympathize.

AUDIENCE: Speak to us Lord!
READER 1: Be not like a horse or a mule,
READER 2: without understanding;
READER 1: which must be curbed,
READER 2: with bit and bridle.
AUDIENCE: Speak to us, your servants will hear!

10

Promise for a New Year

Scriptural Base: Joel 1, 2
Subject: Judgment, Repentance, Deliverance

Background of the Selection

The "Day of the Lord" has had various reception in this world. Some have seen the idea of a day of judgment as just so much pessimistic talk or doomsday-ism. Others have taken heed, reformed and then been disappointed that their expectations were dashed when God did not carry out what their prophet or interpretation had suggested. But there is truth in the doctrine and prophecies of judgment. In the Old Testament the Day of the Lord was a notion that summed up all expectations of God's people regarding his deliverance. In this sense Christians have always seen profound meaning for the salvific action of God in judgment. Judgment is after all a declaration that God's people have chosen the right side of the controversy between and evil. In this reading we see judgment as a promise of deliverance.

Ideas for Reading

Participants: READER 1, READER 2, READER 3 and AUDIENCE 1, AUDIENCE 2, AUDIENCE 3, AUDIENCE 4.

The AUDIENCE should be arbitrarily divided up by the worship leader. Obviously it is crucial that people know clearly what part of the AUDIENCE they will be in if they are to experience the full effects of their participation.

Promise for a New Year

READER 1: Hear this—
READER 2: This is the word of the Lord!
READER 3: Listen to this—
ALL READERS: All you church people!

READER 1: Tell it to your children—
READER 2: Let your children tell it to their children—
READER 3: And let their children tell it to their next generation.

READER 1: A nation has invaded my land—
READER 2: A nation powerful and without number—
READER 3: A nation with the teeth of a lion—
READER 1: A nation with the fangs of a lioness.
ALL READERS: Joy has withered away.

AUDIENCE 3: Mourn!
AUDIENCE 1: Wail!
AUDIENCE 2: Spend the night in sackcloth!
AUDIENCE 4: Declare a holy fast!
AUDIENCE 3: Call a sacred assembly!
AUDIENCE 1: Summon all who live in the land!
ALL: Cry out to the Lord!!

READER 1: The day of the Lord is near!
AUDIENCE 3: Blow the trumpet in Zion!
AUDIENCE 4: Sound the alarm!
READER 1: At the very sight of this army, nations are in anguish
READER 2: Every face turns pale!
READER 1: God's soldiers will rush upon the city.

AUDIENCE 3: Let all who live in the land tremble
AUDIENCE 1: For the day of the Lord is coming.
ALL: It is close at hand.

READER 1: With a noise like that of chariots—
READER 2: God leaps over the mountain tops!

READER 1: Like a crackling fire consuming stubble—
READER 3: God's mighty army is drawn up for battle!

READER 1: At the very sight of this army, nations are in anguish—
READER 2: Every face turns pale!
READER 1: God's soldiers will rush upon the city.
READER 3: They will run along the wall!

AUDIENCE 2: They will climb into the houses—
AUDIENCE 4: Like thieves they will enter through the windows.

READER 1: The Lord thunders at the head of his army
READER 2: His forces are beyond number,
READER 3: And mighty are those who obey his command.
READER 1: Return to me with all your heart—
READER 2: With fasting and weeping and mourning!
READER 3: Rend your hearts and not your garments.

AUDIENCE 1: Return to the Lord your God—
AUDIENCE 3: For he is gracious and compassionate—
AUDIENCE 1: Slow to anger—
AUDIENCE 4: Abounding in love.
AUDIENCE 1: He may turn
AUDIENCE 2: And have pity
AUDIENCE 3: And leave behind a blessing.

READER 1: Blow the trumpet in Zion!
READER 2 Declare a holy fast!
READER 3 Call a sacred assembly.
AUDIENCE 1: Gather the people!
AUDIENCE 2: Consecrate the assembly!
AUDIENCE 3: Bring together the elders!
AUDIENCE 4: Gather the children!

READER 1: Let the priests weep
READER 3: between the temple porch and the altar.
READER 2: Let them say,
READER 3: Spare your people, O Lord.

READER 1: Then the Lord will be jealous
READER 3: for his land and take pity on his people.
READER 2: Then the Lord will satisfy you fully.

AUDIENCE 3: Be glad, O people of Zion!
AUDIENCE 2: Rejoice in the Lord your God!
READER 1: He has given you the autumn rains in righteousness.
READER 2: He sends you abundant showers.

AUDIENCE 4: We will eat
READER 3: Until we are full
AUDIENCE 1: We will praise the name of the Lord your God
READER 2: He has worked wonders for you.
READER 1: Never again will my people be shamed.

READER 3: Then you will know that I am in Israel
READER 1: That I am the Lord your God
READER 2: That there is no other
ALL READERS: Never again will my people be shamed.

READER 1: And everyone who calls on the name of the Lord
READER 2: will be saved
ALL: There will be deliverance.

11

Rich Young Ruler

Scriptural Base: Matthew 19:16–22
Subject: Attitudes, Response to Christ, God's Expectations

Background of the Selection

The story of the rich young ruler puts wealth and service in proper perspective. Jesus carefully unmasks the young man by making him choose between a life of service and a life of self. Unfortunately the man left Jesus disappointed, understanding that eternal life was an attitude and not a condition, yet unwilling to make the commitment. Salvation is portrayed as a human impossibility—as impossible as a camel crawling through an eye of a needle. Once we accept God's salvation we find our attitude and relationship to each other changes.

Ideas for Reading

Participants: READER 1, READER 2, and AUDIENCE.

Place the READERS on either side of the platform full face to the congregation. Alert the AUDIENCE to at least two places in the reading. In one place the AUDIENCE just shakes their heads. In another place the AUDIENCE gives out a sigh. It would be wise to practice these briefly before reading.

Rich Young Ruler

READER 1: A certain rich—
READER 2: And *very* young ruler—
READER 1: once posed this question to Jesus:
AUDIENCE: Good Teacher—
READER 1: Why do you call me good?
READER 2: There is only one who is good.
AUDIENCE: Master—
READER 1: No one is good except God.
AUDIENCE: What must I do—
READER 2: You have read the commandments—
AUDIENCE: To inherit eternal life?

READER 1: Have you kept the commandments?
AUDIENCE: Yes, yes!
READER 2: What about adultery?
AUDIENCE: I haven't committed—
READER 1: What about murdering?
AUDIENCE: No, I haven't—
READER 2: What about lying?
AUDIENCE: No, no, no, I don't—
READER 1: What about honoring parents?
AUDIENCE: I do! I do!
READER 2: Good!
READER 1: Good!

READER 2: But—
ALL READERS: You still lack one thing:
READER 1: To keep the commandments!
AUDIENCE: I have kept the commandments!

READER 1: Sell what you have.
AUDIENCE: Sell?
READER 2: Sell!
READER 1: Give to the poor!
AUDIENCE: Give?

READER 2: Give!
AUDIENCE: *[Shake head 4 times and say nothing]*.

READER 1: It is difficult for you
READER 2: who are rich
READER 1: and increased in goods
READER 2: and need nothing—
READER 1: To enter the kingdom of God!
READER 2: In fact—
READER 1: In fact, it is easier,
READER 2: for a camel to crawl
READER 1: through the eye of a needle,
READER 2: than for a rich man,
READER 1: who seems to need nothing,
READER 2: to walk into heaven
READER 1: loaded with riches.
AUDIENCE: **But camels don't crawl.**

READER 2: Then you are wondering—
AUDIENCE: **Riches are from God!**
READER 1: Who can be saved?
READER 2: Those who put God before
READER 1: homes,
READER 2: family,
READER 1: and money—
AUDIENCE: **Impossible!**

READER 1: Will have eternal life
READER 2: and they will also have
READER 1: home,
READER 2: family,
READER 1: and money.
AUDIENCE: *[Let out a disgusted 'sigh']*.

READER 1: Hear the conclusion—
READER 2: About wealth, camels, and eternal life.
READER 1: The certain rich
READER 2: and *very* young ruler—

READER 1: Went away sorrowful,
READER 2: not believing,
READER 1: but proving
READER 2: the words of Jesus.
READER 1: Camels don't crawl!
READER 2: Rich don't sell or give!
READER 1: Nor do they understand
READER 2: that the impossibility of eternal life
READER 1: is possible!
READER 2: But only in Christ.

12

We Rule Because God is Majestic

Scriptural Base: Psalm 8:1–9
Subject: Gratitude, Human Responsibility, God's Grace, God's Greatness

Background of the Selection

The Psalms continually give adoration, honor and praise to the creator God. But Psalm 8 puts humanity into this creation, not just as a participant, but also as a ruler—a ruler who has been crowned with glory and honor. This thought is in keeping with God's word to Adam and Eve in Genesis 1:28, "Be fruitful and increase in number; fill the earth and subdue it. Rule over the fish of the sea and the birds of the air and every living creature that moves on the ground." The New Testament takes us to the end of history when the righteous will reign forever in a recreated earth (Revelation 21–22). The Gospel reveals that in Jesus Christ we are appointed priests and crowned rulers. The value and expectation God places on human beings is well worth our meditation and reading.

Ideas for Reading

Participants: READER 1, READER 2, and AUDIENCE.

The READERS need to be separated from one another and use separate microphones. Call attention to the underlined words and punctuation marks in the AUDIENCE responses. In particular, note that the word "silence" is to be read in a whisper.

Man Rules Because God is Majestic

READER 1: Lord, the Lord God—
READER 2: Is majestic—
READER 1: Is majestic in all the earth!
READER 2: He has set his glory above the heavens.
AUDIENCE: Praise to the glory of the Lord!
READER 1: Praise is chanted
READER 2: by the lips of children and infants.
AUDIENCE: Silence! *[spoken quietly as in a whisper]*

READER 1: Consider the heavens.
READER 2: Consider the work of God's fingers.
READER 1: Consider the moon and the stars—
READER 2: which God has set in place.
AUDIENCE: But has God considered me?
READER 1: God is mindful of you.
AUDIENCE: But who am I?
READER 2: That God should care for you?
AUDIENCE: What has God done for me?
READER 1: He made you a little lower than the heavenly beings,
READER 2: but He has crowned you with glory and honor.
AUDIENCE: I am crowned with glory and honor?

READER 1: He has made you a ruler
READER 2: over the works of his hand.
READER 1: He has put everything under your feet!
AUDIENCE: Then I am a ruler!
READER 2: You are a ruler.
READER 1: You rule over flocks and herds,
READER 2: over beasts of the field—

AUDIENCE: I rule over all that?
READER 1: And—
READER 2: The birds of the air,
READER 1: the fish of the sea,
READER 2: all that swim in the seas—

AUDIENCE: God has made me a ruler?
READER 2: Over all the earth and the fullness thereof.

READER 1: God's name is majestic.
READER 2: The Lord is majestic
READER 1: in all the earth!
READER 2: He is great because He has allowed
AUDIENCE: me to rule the earth?
READER 2: Yes!
READER 1: The Lord
READER 2: crowned you—
READER 1: Crowned you with glory and honor,
READER 2: by having you rule the earth.
AUDIENCE: I am a ruler?…I am a ruler!

13

Who Is The Greatest?

Scriptural Base: Matthew 18:1–4; Mark 9:33–37; Luke 9:46–48
Subject: True Greatness, Service, Altruism, Ethics of the Kingdom

Background of the Selection

Many Christian values are comprehensible only if one first understands Christ's definition of "greatness." At the heart of the Christian ethic is the notion that "the first shall be last and the last shall be first" in the Kingdom of God. This is the Christian ethic of altruism (being motivated by the needs of other people). This reading stresses Christ's teaching on greatness by recounting the story he told in response to the disciples' argumentative question, "Who is the greatest in the kingdom."

Ideas for Reading

Participants: READER 1, READER 2, and AUDIENCE.

In this reading the AUDIENCE is responding to the words of Jesus concerning greatness. The READERS are giving the words and thoughts of Jesus with the AUDIENCE responding. Separate the READERS on the platform.

Who Is The Greatest?

READER 1: One day Jesus' disciples were arguing

READER 2: over which of them would be the greatest in his kingdom.

AUDIENCE: Who is the greatest?

READER 1: Knowing their thoughts

READER 2: Jesus stood a little child beside him.

READER 1: If you welcome this little child in my name

READER 2: you welcome me.

AUDIENCE: Welcome, Lord!

READER 1: If you welcome me

READER 2: you welcome the one who sent me.

AUDIENCE: Welcome, Father!

READER 1: Whoever is least among you all,

READER 2: whoever is like this child,

ALL: He is the greatest!

READER 1: If we think we are really something when we are nothing

READER 2: We deceive ourselves.

AUDIENCE: Who is the greatest?

READER 1: All who are completely humble.

READER 2: All who are completely gentle.

READER 1: All who are completely patient.

READER 2: All who bear with one another in love.

AUDIENCE: They are the greatest?

READER 1: Whoever wants to become great among you

READER 2: must be your servant.

AUDIENCE: Your servant?

READER 1: Whoever wants to be first

READER 2: must be a slave of all.

AUDIENCE: A slave?

READER 1: Those who exalt themselves will be humbled.

READER 2: Those who humble themselves will be exalted.

AUDIENCE: They are the greatest?

READER 1: Take pride in yourself

READER 2: but do it without comparing yourself to others.

READER 1: Take pride in yourself
READER 2: but show it by learning to carry your own load.
AUDIENCE: Take *pride* in yourself?
READER 1: You are God's chosen people.
READER 2: You are holy, set apart by God for a righteous purpose.
READER 1: You are loved by God—
READER 2: You matter to God!
AUDIENCE: Take *pride* in yourself.

READER 1: Clothe yourself with compassion.
READER 2: Clothe yourself with kindness.
AUDIENCE: Take *pride* in yourself.
READER 1: Clothe yourself with humility.
READER 2: Clothe yourself with gentleness.
READER 1: Clothe yourself with patience.
READER 2: *Because* you are God's chosen people!
AUDIENCE: I am *holy* and dearly *loved* by God!

READER 1: Remember—
READER 2: Students are not above their teacher.
AUDIENCE: Yes, I know that! That is right!
READER 1: And those who are genuinely educated—
READER 2: Will be like their teacher.

AUDIENCE: That is right! That is absolutely right!
READER 1: Surely he took up our infirmities
READER 2: and carried our sorrows.
READER 1: He was pierced for our transgressions.
READER 2: He was crushed for our iniquities.
AUDIENCE: The first shall be last.

READER 1: He will see his offspring and prolong his days
READER 2: and the will of the Lord will prosper in his hand.
AUDIENCE: The last shall be first.
READER 1: He was oppressed and afflicted,
READER 2: yet he did not open his mouth.
READER 1: He was led like a lamb
READER 2: to the slaughter

READER 1: and as a sheep before her shearers are silent,
READER 2: he did not open his mouth.
AUDIENCE: We will be like our *teacher*.

READER 1: Remember, two are better than one.
READER 2: If one falls down his friend can help him up.
AUDIENCE: Help him up.
READER 1: Pity the person who falls
READER 2: and has no one to help!
AUDIENCE: Help!

READER 1: He shall see the light of life and be satisfied.
READER 2: His righteousness will justify many.
READER 1: He will bear their iniquities.
READER 2: He gave his life unto death.
ALL: *He* is the greatest!

14

The New Heart

Scriptural Base: Ezekiel 11:14–25; Ezekiel 36:22–32
Subject: Deliverance, Conversion, Salvation

Background of the Selection

The Scriptures are Christ-centered from beginning to end. The message God sends his believers is wrapped up in the promise for divine deliverance. The Old Testament narrative presents God as a delivering God. The New Testament interprets these deliverance acts as the works of divine activity centered in Jesus Christ. With this deliverance from enemies, powers and places, comes deliverance from the total dominance of the "old man of sin," that is, our depravity and evil desires. A new heart is promised to those who wish to be delivered. This new heart does not simply empower believers to reach their goals. The new heart alters these goals. In this reading we will meditate on the new heart theme of Ezekiel 11 and 36.

Ideas for Reading

Participants: READER 1, READER 2, READER 3, and AUDIENCE.

The AUDIENCE is responding as the people who have gone astray. They have been beaten by the enemy and they are sitting in captivity without their land. They have been humbled. The READERS are giving the message of God to the people.

The New Heart

READER 1: Hear what the Sovereign Lord says.
READER 2: I will gather you from the nations.
READER 3: I will bring you back from the countries,
READER 2: where you have been scattered
READER 1: and return your land.
AUDIENCE: What will we do, Lord?

READER 1: You will return to the land.
READER 2: You will remove all your vile images
READER 3: and detestable idols.
AUDIENCE: But we love them, Lord.
READER 2: I know.
READER 1: I know.

READER 1: But in my faithfulness to you
READER 2: I will give you an undivided heart,
READER 3: I will put a new Spirit in you,
READER 2: I will remove your heart of stone,
READER 1: and give you a heart of flesh.
AUDIENCE: What good will that do?

READER 1: Because of that you will follow my decrees
READER 2: and you will find it more natural
READER 3: to be careful to keep my laws.
READER 2: For you will be my people.
READER 1: And I will be your God.
AUDIENCE: What if we don't want that?
READER 1: For those whose hearts are devoted to their vile images
READER 2: and detestable idols,
READER 3: I will bring down on their own heads what they have done.
AUDIENCE: Is that a threat?
READER 2: Yes—
READER 1: You could look at it that way.

READER 1: Or you could be wise and learn from it.
READER 2: It could be seen as information.

AUDIENCE: Explain yourself, Lord.
READER 3: You could see it as a promise
READER 2: A promise—
READER 1: Of deliverance!
AUDIENCE: Of deliverance?!

READER 1: When my people lived in their own land
READER 2: they defiled it
READER 3: by their conduct—their actions,
READER 2: so I poured out my wrath.
AUDIENCE: We know!
READER 1: Of course, you know.

READER 1: Which do you detest more
READER 2: my wrath?
READER 3: or my actions?
READER 2: There is a connection, you know
READER 1: between your hardship and your wickedness.
AUDIENCE: We are learning, Lord.

READER 1: Because of your unfaithfulness to me
READER 2: you tested my faithfulness to you.
READER 3: And I let you know
READER 2: what it would be like
READER 1: to live without me.
AUDIENCE: We are thick between the ears, Lord.

READER 1: You lived without me
READER 2: and you got beat up
READER 3: by the world.
AUDIENCE: Yes!
READER 2: The world without me,
READER 1: is not a friendly place.

READER 1: Everybody knows you now!
READER 2: Yes—everybody knows you now!
READER 3: They all know that you are my people
READER 2: and because you were unfaithful

READER 1: you lost your land.
AUDIENCE: Everybody knows us now.

READER 1: But it was not the witness I wanted.
READER 2: I wanted them to know my faithfulness
READER 3: Not your faithlessness!
AUDIENCE: So, what now, Lord?
READER 2: Will you try again
READER 1: Now that you have learned?

READER 1: I will take you out of the world
READER 2: and gather you back to your own.
READER 3: I will sprinkle you clean.
READER 2: I will remove your heart of stone'
READER 1: I will give you a heart of flesh.
AUDIENCE: What will we do?
READER 1: You will remember your evil ways and wicked deeds—
READER 2: You will loathe those sins you commit.
READER 3: You will know my faithfulness.
READER 2: You will act out of your new heart.
READER 1: You will be my witnesses.
AUDIENCE: And everybody will know *you* through us!

15

Teach Us To Pray

Scriptural Base: Matthew 6:7–15; Matthew: 7–12; Luke 11:5–11
Subject: Prayer, God's Willingness to Bless, God's Wisdom, Our Needs

Background of the selection

Jesus' disciples asked him just how they were to pray. His sample prayer and the New Testament stories surrounding prayer not only told the disciples how to pray but also how to live their lives. In the appropriate living of life Jesus answered people's prayers. Some have suggested that our works of faith are indicative of our seriousness in our prayer to God. In part this was what Jesus was teaching us when he instructed us how to pray. This reading underscores not only the words of Jesus but also the reaction on the part of God toward prayer. Thus we receive a revelation of God's character as well.

Ideas for Reading

Participants: READER 1, READER 2, and AUDIENCE.

The AUDIENCE assumes the position of the disciples in this reading, and as such needs to reflect, in their voices, an earnest desire for answers. The READERS should be separated on the platform and be full face to the audience looking directly into their faces. The reading is a dialogue between humanity and God

Teach Us To Pray

READER 1: After Jesus had finished praying one day,
READER 2: one of his disciples asked him,
READER 1: Lord, would you teach us to pray?
READER 2: And Jesus taught them saying,
READER 1: When you pray, say: Father,
READER 2: hallowed be your name,
READER 1: your kingdom come,
READER 2: your will be done in earth and heaven.
AUDIENCE: Teach us to pray.

READER 1: Then ask—
AUDIENCE: Give us each day our daily bread.
READER 2: and it will be given to you.
READER 1: Then seek—
AUDIENCE: Forgive us the wrong we have done.
READER 2: And you will find forgiveness.
READER 1: Then knock—
AUDIENCE: Lead us not into temptation.
READER 2: And temptation's door will be closed.
READER 1: Then seek again—
AUDIENCE: Deliver us from the power of evil.
READER 2: And I will give you authority to stand.

AUDIENCE: Lord, teach us to pray.
READER 1: Ask!
AUDIENCE: And it will be given.
READER 2: Seek!
AUDIENCE: And you will find.
READER 1: Knock!
AUDIENCE: And the door will opened to you.
READER 2: Whoever asks—
AUDIENCE: Receives!
READER 1: Whoever seeks—
AUDIENCE: Finds!
READER 2: And whoever knocks—

AUDIENCE: Perceives an open door.
ALL READERS: Lord, teach us to pray.

READER 1: Prayer is something like talking to a friend.
READER 2: You ask him for help.
AUDIENCE: Some relatives just dropped in for a visit.
READER 1: You seek him in your need.
AUDIENCE: I don't have enough food to set before him.
READER 2: You knock on your friend's door for help.
AUDIENCE: Could you help me out?
READER 1: You knock confidently—
READER 2: And he says, I've already gone to bed!
READER 1: You seek boldly—
READER 2: I know it's not convenient, but I'm desperate.
READER 1: You ask persistently—
AUDIENCE: Could you help me out?...*Please* help me out?
READER 1: And your friend gets up and brings you the food!
READER 2: If even irritated people can give good gifts
READER 1: when they believe you are serious,
READER 2: don't you think God is even more willing
READER 1: to grant you your needs?
AUDIENCE: Lord, teach *us* to pray.

READER 1: Prayer is something like talking to your parents.
AUDIENCE: I need a fish.
READER 2: And you get a *fish,*
READER 1: not a *snake!*
AUDIENCE: I need an *egg.*
READER 2: And you get a *egg.*
READER 1: not a *scorpion!*
READER 2: You knock on his door—
AUDIENCE: I need a loaf of *bread.*
READER 1: And you get *bread.*
READER 2: not a *stone!*
READER 1: If human fathers, who are not sinless
READER 2: know how to give good gifts,
READER 1: how much more will your heavenly Father

READER 2: give the Holy Spirit to those who ask him!
AUDIENCE: Teach us to *pray*.

READER 1: When you pray; ask, seek, and knock,
READER 2: and your Father in heaven
AUDIENCE: will give good gifts,
READER 2: not scorpions,
READER 1: or snakes,
READER 2: or stones,
READER 1: but His Spirit.
READER 2: When you pray,
READER 1: say,
READER 2: Father, hallowed be your name—
READER 1: It is your kingdom—
READER 2: It is your power—
READER 1: It is to your glory—
READER 2: That we want to learn how to pray,
ALL: Forever, Amen!

16

Gratitude

Scriptural Base: Selected Old and New Testament Passages
Subject: Praise, Thanksgiving, Gratitude

Background of the Selection

Gratitude is first an attitude and then an expression. According to the Scriptures, the Gospel stimulates genuine gratitude. We are in a serious condition which modern writers often call "estrangement." In this condition one experiences hostility, separation, and disconnection not only from each other, but within ourselves. The word of God makes it clear that separation from God can only be solved by reconciliation in Jesus Christ. Because God loved us and demonstrated that love in Jesus Christ, we can love ourselves and others.

This reading emphasizes that our treatment of others gives evidence of our appreciation of God. We have two natures: "spirit" and "flesh" and what we do, or how we act, has much to do with "feeding" one or the other of those natures. We need reminding of the reasons for which we are grateful. Scripture is generous in such reminders. Reading them affirms our decision to respond to God positively.

Ideas for Reading

Participants: READER 1, READER 2, and AUDIENCE 1, 2, 3.

The READER will stand in front on each side of the platform. The AUDIENCE is the congregation or anyone else involved in the reading. For this reading you will need to divide the AUDIENCE is divided into three parts.

Gratitude

READER 1: Give thanks to the Lord,
READER 2: call on his name.
AUDIENCE 1: Make known among the nations
AUDIENCE 2: what he has done.
AUDIENCE 3: Give thanks to the Lord.
ALL READERS: For he is good—
ALL AUDIENCE: And his love endures forever.

AUDIENCE 1: With what shall we praise him?
READER 1: With trumpets and songs,
READER 2: with cymbals and harps,
AUDIENCE 1: with voices and choirs,
AUDIENCE 2: with other instruments,
AUDIENCE 3: with sacrifices.
ALL READERS: For he is good—
ALL AUDIENCE: And his love endures forever.

AUDIENCE 2: Why should we thank him?
READER 1: Because he is our strength and shield!
READER 2: Because our hearts leap for joy!
AUDIENCE 1: We cannot be silent.
AUDIENCE 2: We must tell
AUDIENCE 3: of his wonderful deeds.
ALL READERS: For he is good—
ALL AUDIENCE: And his love endures forever.

AUDIENCE 3: When shall we praise him?
READER 1: Enter his gates with thanksgiving.
READER 2: Enter his courts with praise.
AUDIENCE 1: Let the sound of singing
AUDIENCE 2: ever be on your lips.
AUDIENCE 3: Give him thanks constantly.
ALL READERS: For he is good—
ALL AUDIENCE: And his love endures forever.

READER 1: Thank him for his righteous laws.
READER 2: Thank him for becoming our salvation.
READER 1: Like the voices of bride and bridegroom,
READER 2: like the voices of the penitent,
AUDIENCE 1: like those in triumphal procession,
AUDIENCE 2: like those eating loaves and fishes,
AUDIENCE 3: like those at the last supper—
ALL READERS: Give him thanks—
ALL AUDIENCE: For he is good forever.

READER 1: Jesus took the five loaves and two fishes
AUDIENCE 1: But first he gave thanks.
READER 2: Jesus took the bread and the wine
AUDIENCE 2: But first he gave thanks.
READER 1: Jesus fed them at Tiberias—
AUDIENCE 3: But first he gave thanks.

ALL AUDIENCE: How do we show gratitude?
READER 1: By thanking God for our food.
READER 2: By thanking God for our trials.
READER 1: By resisting a foolish heart.
READER 2: By participating in the Lord's Supper.
READER 1: By accepting Christ's victory.
READER 2: By showing generosity.
READER 1: By rejecting foolish talk.
READER 2: By shunning obscenity.
READER 1: By avoiding coarse jokes.

AUDIENCE 3: Everywhere and in everything—
READER 1: Make your requests known to God—
READER 2: Through thanksgiving.
READER 1: He has become our salvation.
READER 2: He shares the inheritance of the saints.

AUDIENCE 1: Praise,
AUDIENCE 2: Glory,
AUDIENCE 3: Wisdom,
AUDIENCE 2: Thanks,

AUDIENCE 1: Honor,
AUDIENCE 2: Power,
AUDIENCE 3: Strength—
READER 1: Be to our God
READER 2: Forever and ever.

READER 1: We give thanks to you,
READER 2: Lord God Almighty.
READER 1: Because you have taken your great power
READER 2: and have begun to reign—
ALL AUDIENCE: And your love endures forever.

17

The Joy of Forgiving

Scriptural Base: Selected Old and New Testament Passages
Subject: Forgiveness, God's Grace

Background of the Selection

Forgiveness is often hard to grant because of our proclivity to hold grudges, nurse personal wounds, and harbor self-sorrow. But in the act of forgiving, as well as in the receiving of forgiveness, there is a joy that can only be experienced. There is a release and fulfillment, there is relief and freedom. Refusing to forgive is a form of bondage and self-slavery. The Bible is replete with illustrations of the personal experience of forgiveness, but these are simply reenactments of God's forgiveness of us. It is the scriptural position that without God's forgiveness none of us would be motivated or able to forgive others. This reading will stress that fact.

Ideas for Reading

Participants: READER 1, READER 2, AUDIENCE divided into: LEFT, MIDDLE, RIGHT, MEN, WOMEN, OVER 40 YEARS OF AGE, UNDER 40 YEARS OF AGE. There will be a dynamic that is impressive and exciting, but rehearsing will be a necessity. Done right this reading will produce a "wave" effect throughout your AUDIENCE and will certainly command everyone's attention.

READERS 1 and 2 should be separated on the platform—one on each side. Since most congregations are not accustomed to responding very energetically, you may need to rehearse them a bit too. Encourage your AUDIENCE to say their lines with feelings. We repeat: You will need to practice with your READERS and your AUDIENCE.

The Joy of Forgiving

READER 1: When Joseph's brothers saw that their father was dead,
READER 2: they said,
LEFT: **What if Joseph holds a grudge against us**
MIDDLE: **and pays us back**
RIGHT: **for all the wrongs we did to him?**
READER 2: So they send word to Joseph saying,
READER 1: Our father Jacob left these instructions before he died:
READER 2: This is what you are to say to your brother Joseph:
LEFT: **I ask you to forgive your brothers.**
MIDDLE: **Forgive them**
READER 1: of their sins in treating you so badly.
RIGHT: **Forgive them**
READER 2: of the wrongs they have committed against you.
LEFT: **Forgive them**
READER 1: for they are servants
READER 2: of the God of your father.
ALL: **Forgive them!**

READER 1: And when the message came to him
READER 2: Joseph wept.
READER 1: He spoke kindly to them
READER 2: and assured them of his forgiveness.
ALL: **He forgave them.**

READER 1: The Lord is slow to anger, abounding in love,
READER 2: forgiving sin and rebellion.
WOMEN: **He forgives.**
MEN: **He hears us from heaven.**
OVER 40: **He watches from his dwelling place.**
UNDER 40: **And when he hears**
ALL: **He forgives.**

READER 1: He is forgiving God.
READER 2: He is gracious and compassionate.
MEN: **He is slow to anger,**
WOMEN: **abounding in love!**

ALL: He forgives.
READER 1: If my people,
READER 2: who are called by my name,
LEFT: will humble themselves
RIGHT: and pray
MIDDLE: and seek my face
MEN: and turn from their wicked ways,
WOMEN: then I will hear from heaven—
ALL: And I will forgive their sin.

READER 1: Help us, 0 God our Savior,
MIDDLE: for the glory of your name;
READER 2: Deliver us, 0 Lord our God
LEFT: in your forgiving ways.
READER 1: Who is a God like you
READER 2: who pardons and forgives
READER 1: the transgression of the remnant?
RIGHT: Forgive us our debts—
ALL: As we have forgiven our debtors.

READER 1: Do you like to be judged?
RIGHT: No!
READER 2: Then don't judge.
READER 1: Do you like to be condemned?
LEFT: No!
READER 2: Then don't condemn.
READER 1: Do you like to be forgiven?
MIDDLE: Yes!
ALL: Then forgive!

READER 1: Forgive and you will be forgiven.
MEN: Be kind.
WOMEN: Be compassionate.
LEFT: Forgive each other,
RIGHT: just as in Christ God forgave you.
ALL: Forgive as the Lord forgave you.

18

The Pearl

Scriptural Base: Matthew 13:45–46
Subject: God's Faithfulness to Humankind, Our Worth, God's Grace

Background of the Selection

It has been said that Jesus was not a theologian but God who told stories! The two short stories of the pearl and the hidden treasure are examples of Jesus' stories that have transcended the ages. A careful reading of the text indicates that we are the treasure and the pearl that Jesus came to earth to find. Jesus' words were given to the masses in Judea and Galilee who had come to believe that only the religious leaders had access to God. These two short stories challenge that idea. The reading is structured to tell the story again and to emphasize that the rank and file in church seats are pearls and treasures in God's eyes. And as we come to recognize the value God places upon us we will come to believe the fact of God's transforming love.

Ideas for Reading

Participants: READER 1, READER 2, and AUDIENCE.

The READERS need to be placed on either side of the rostrum for the best effect. The AUDIENCE needs to pay close attention to punctuation and italicized words. Note the lines in which the word "pearl" is used. These lines probably need to be practiced before the reading is done in its entirety.

The Pearl

READER 1: The kingdom of heaven
READER 2: is like a man finding a treasure hidden in a field.
READER 1: The kingdom of heaven
READER 2: is like a merchant looking for fine pearls.

AUDIENCE: The kingdom of heaven, where is it?
READER 1: The kingdom of heaven
READER 2: is within you
READER 1: and around you.

AUDIENCE: The kingdom of heaven, when is it?
READER 1: The kingdom of heaven
READER 2: is right now,
READER 1: today
READER 2: and tomorrow
READER 1: and forever.

AUDIENCE: But what is the kingdom like?
READER 1: The kingdom of heaven
READER 2: is like a farmer who finds a treasure hidden in his field.
READER 1: The kingdom of heaven
READER 2: is like an entrepreneur looking for fine pearls.
READER 1: Now do you understand?

AUDIENCE: I understand, but—
READER 1: But what it is like?
READER 2: You don't understand.
AUDIENCE: I don't understand!
READER 1: The kingdom of heaven
READER 2: is about a farmer who mortgages his farm
READER 1: in order to buy a field with treasure buried in it.
READER 2: The kingdom of heaven
READER 1: is about an entrepreneur who takes out a second mortgage
READER 2: in order to buy a pearl of great worth.

AUDIENCE: So—
READER 1: *You* are the treasure.
AUDIENCE: I am the treasure?
READER 1: You are the *sought-after* treasure.
AUDIENCE: I am the *treasure!*
READER 2: You are the treasure.

AUDIENCE: And—
READER 2: You are the pearl.
AUDIENCE: *I* am the pearl?
READER 1: You are the costly pearl of great worth.
AUDIENCE: I am the *pearl!*
READER 2: *You are the pearl!*

AUDIENCE: Then the kingdom of heaven cares about me?
READER 1: The kingdom sends a man
READER 2: to buy the *sought-after* treasure!
READER 1: The kingdom sends an entrepreneur to purchase
READER 2: the costly pearl of great worth.
AUDIENCE: I am the *treasure!* I am the *pearl!*

READER 1: So in the kingdom of heaven
READER 2: you matter!
READER 1: Within and without,
READER 2: today and tomorrow.

READER 1: You matter to God!
READER 2: He comes searching.
READER 1: The kingdom is
READER 2: about Christ,
READER 1: who buys
READER 2: pearls and treasures.

19

Favoritism Forbidden

Scriptural Base: James 2:1–14
Subject: Partiality, Favoritism, Thoughtfulness, Acceptance

Background of the Selection

Jesus' greatest concern throughout the New Testament is not with theology or doctrine but with the behavior of those who claimed to be members of the Kingdom of God. He was concerned about how we treat each other. Indeed, Jesus had the harshest words to say to people who treated each other unkindly. We worship God by treating each other as we would wish to be treated. The book of James concerns itself with duties and responsibilities to each other, including the family. Loving each other means translating talk to action.

Ideas for Reading

Participants: READER 1, READER 2, and AUDIENCE.

The AUDIENCE plays the part of the Pharisee in this reading and should respond to the READERS in a very matter-of-fact manner. The READERS need to show concern and intensity in their voices, making the matter-of-fact responses even more cool and uncaring. The READERS should be separated and read directly to the audience.

Favoritism Forbidden

READER 1: Suppose—
READER 2: Just suppose—
READER 1: A man coming into your meeting
READER 2: was wearing fine clothes.
AUDIENCE: Offer him a seat!

READER 1: Suppose—
READER 2: Just suppose—
READER 1: A man coming into your meeting
READER 2: was wearing fine clothes *and* a gold ring.
AUDIENCE: Offer him a seat, of course!

READER 1: Would you say to him
READER 2: "You stand over there?"
AUDIENCE: No!
READER 1: Or ask him to sit on the floor?
AUDIENCE: Of course not!

READER 2: Now suppose—
READER 1: Just suppose—
READER 2: A man coming into your meeting
READER 1: was wearing shabby clothes and had *no* gold ring.
READER 2: Where would you seat him?
AUDIENCE: That's different!

READER 1: Where would you seat him?
READER 2: Where would you seat him?
AUDIENCE: In the back.
READER 2: Or—
AUDIENCE: On the floor.
READER 1: Or—
AUDIENCE: I may not even let him in.

READER 1: You have favored those who exploit you,
READER 2: those who take you to court,

READER 1: those who slander
READER 2: the noble name of Jesus.

READER 1: You see—the kingdom of heaven
READER 2: revolves around those
READER 1: who have done kind things
READER 2: to the least of humanity—
READER 1: Children,
READER 2: the poor,
READER 1: the shabbily dressed
AUDIENCE: and the rich?
READER 2: And the rich if—
READER 1: If you don't want a favor in return.
READER 2: If you do—
READER 1: Then your thoughts are evil.

READER 2: Listen—
READER 1: Who has God chosen to be rich in faith?
AUDIENCE: The man with fine clothes?
READER 2: No!
READER 1: The poor.
READER 2: Who will inherit the kingdom?
AUDIENCE: The man with the gold ring?
READER 1: No!
READER 2: Those who love God.

AUDIENCE: Then have I sinned?
READER 1: By showing favoritism
READER 2: you have sinned—
READER 1: For you have not kept the royal law
READER 2: which says,
READER 1: "Love your neighbor as yourself."

AUDIENCE: How should I speak and act?
READER 1: Speak and act
READER 2: as though you are going to be judged
READER 1: by the law that gives freedom.
AUDIENCE: Judgment? But what of mercy?

READER 2: Judgment triumphs over mercy

READER 1: to anyone who has not been merciful.

READER 2: But—

READER 1: If you treat

READER 2: the poor,

READER 1: the children,

READER 2: the shabbily dressed—

AUDIENCE: And the rich?

READER 1: As you would want to be treated

READER 2: by showing mercy,

READER 1: then—

READER 2: Mercy triumphs over judgment.

READER 1: In that you have done it to the least of these

READER 2: you have done unto Jesus.

20

Didache for the Tongue

Scriptural Base: James 3; Philippians 1:27
Subject: Words, Power of Words, Affirming, Encouraging, Gossip, Slander

Background of the Selection

Didache is the Greek word for "teaching." The New Testament writers anticipate the danger and recognize the potential blessing of the words we utter with our tongues. Because of this extraordinary power, the "tongue" is to be kept under the control of the kingly and sanctified power of reason. It is like a rudder on a big ship that is capable of guiding the boat through rough or mild seas. Of course, the tongue only does what the brain instructs it to do, but the focus on the tongue as such a small part of the body is an intriguing subject for the scriptural writers. In this reading we are reminded of the tongue's power as depicted in the book of James. This is indeed a "teaching" for the tongue—some wonderful imperatives for those who love harmony in relationship.

Ideas for Reading

Participants: READER 1, READER 2, and AUDIENCE.

In this reading the AUDIENCE is supporting the assertions and imperatives of the READERS. They are affirming that what God says about controlling the tongue is wise and enhances more meaningful community. Encourage them to feel how warm that affirmation can be, and especially how warm the results of a controlled tongue can be.

Didache for the Tongue

READER 1: We all stumble in many ways.

READER 2: If anyone were never at fault, we would say,

AUDIENCE: there is a perfect person.

READER 1: If some people were never at fault, we say,

AUDIENCE: those people are able to keep themselves in check.

READER 2: But we all stumble at least in *little* ways.

READER 1: A bit in the mouth of a horse

AUDIENCE: can turn the whole horse.

READER 2: A rudder on the bottom of a boat

AUDIENCE: can turn the whole ship.

READER 1: A tiny spark in the woods

AUDIENCE: can burn up the whole forest.

READER 1: *Likewise*—that tiny tongue in that big body,

READER 2: with its boasting,

READER 1: with its deadly poison,

READER 2: with its slanderings,

READER 1: with its praise—

AUDIENCE: It can corrupt the whole being!

READER 1: With the tongue we *praise* our Lord and Father.

READER 2: With the tongue we *curse* people made in God's likeness.

READER 1: Out of the same mouth come praise and cursing.

READER 2: My brothers, this should not be.

AUDIENCE: Tame it!

READER 1: The tongue also is a fire.

READER 2: The tongue is a world of evil

READER 1: among the parts of the body.

READER 2: It can corrupt the whole person.

READER 1: It can set the whole course of his life on fire.

AUDIENCE: Tame it!

READER 2: We tame animals.

READER 1: We tame birds.

AUDIENCE: Tame the tongue!

READER 2: We tame reptiles.

READER 1: We tame porpoises
READER 2: and whales.
AUDIENCE: Tame the tongue!!

READER 1: But no man tames the tongue.
READER 2: No man tames the tongue.
AUDIENCE: Tame it! Tame the tongue!!
READER 1: It is a restless evil.
READER 2: It is full of deadly poison.
AUDIENCE: Amen! Tame the tongue!!

READER 1: Do not slander one another.
READER 2: Anyone who speaks against his brother or judges him,
READER 1: speaks against the law and judges it.
READER 2: Anyone who speaks against the law or judges it,
READER 1: speaks against the lawgiver and judges him.
AUDIENCE: There is only one Lawgiver and Judge.

READER 1: Do not let any unwholesome talk come out of your mouths.
READER 2: Let only what is helpful
READER 1: for building others up
READER 2: come out of your mouths.
AUDIENCE: *Encourage* them.
READER 1: Bless those who persecute you.
AUDIENCE: *Bless* them.
READER 2: Rejoice with those who rejoice.
AUDIENCE: *Rejoice* with them.
READER 1: Mourn with those who mourn.
AUDIENCE: *Mourn* with them.

READER 1: Christ Jesus came into the world to save sinners.
READER 2: When people are caught in a sin,
READER 1: restore them gently.
AUDIENCE: Restore him!
READER 2: Carry their burdens.
AUDIENCE: Assist her!

READER 1: Let the word of Christ dwell in you richly.

READER 2: Teach each other.

AUDIENCE: Teach!

READER 1: Admonish one another in wisdom.

AUDIENCE: Admonish!

READER 2: Sing psalms, hymns and spiritual songs.

AUDIENCE: Sing!

READER 2: And let your singing

READER 1: be with gratitude

READER 2: in your hearts to God.

READER 1: Whatever you do in word or deed—

READER 2: Do it all in the name of the Lord Jesus

AUDIENCE: Giving thanks to God the Father through him.

READER 1: If one of you should wander from the truth

READER 2: and someone should bring him back—

AUDIENCE: Remember this!

READER 1: Whoever turns sinners

READER 2: from the error of their way

READER 1: will save them from death

READER 2: and cover over a multitude of sins.

READER 1: Live in harmony

READER 2: with one another.

AUDIENCE: Do not be proud.

READER 1: But be willing to associate

READER 2: with people of low position.

AUDIENCE: Do not be snooty.

READER 1: Do not think of yourself

READER 2: more highly than you ought.

AUDIENCE: Do not be conceited.

READER 1: But rather think of yourself

READER 2: with sober judgment,

READER 1: in accordance with the measure of faith

READER 2: God has given you.

AUDIENCE: Do not seek the praise of others.

READER 1: Seek rather the praise of God.

READER 2: Even the Son of Man did not come

READER 1: to be served, but to serve,
AUDIENCE: He came to serve—
READER 2: And gave his life as a ransom for many.
READER 1: So whatever happens,
READER 2: conduct yourselves in a manner
READER 1: worthy of the Gospel of Christ.
ALL: Tame the tongue!!
READER 2: And tell the world of your salvation!

21

He Will Redeem

Scriptural Base: Psalm 130
Subject: Salvation, Assurance, Faith

Background of the Selection

The story of redemption is the recurring theme in the Psalms. These songs are filled with assurances that the Creator God is faithful to human beings and offers the solution to the sin problem. David himself was convinced that he would ultimately be redeemed in spite of his sinful acts and attitude. This reading progresses from crying for help to the ultimate salvation of those who accept the redemption of God.

Ideas for Reading

Participants: READER 1, READER 2, and AUDIENCE.

The two READERS can be either male or female. We suggest a man and woman to imply God's inclusiveness in salvation. Put the READERS on each corner of the platform using separate microphones. Encourage the AUDIENCE to respond with feeling—as if they were David pleading for the assurance of redemption.

He Will Redeem

READER 1: O Lord, let your ears be attentive

READER 2: to our cry for mercy.

READER 1: Out of the depth,

READER 2: we cry to you, O Lord.

AUDIENCE: Hear our voice.

READER 1: If You—

READER 2: If you, O Lord, kept a record of our sins,

READER 1: Who could stand?

READER 2: But with you—

AUDIENCE: Is there forgiveness?

READER 1: We wait for the Lord.

READER 2: We wait for the Lord.

AUDIENCE: We wait for the Lord.

READER 1: Our souls wait for the Lord.

READER 2: In His word we put our hope.

READER 1: Our souls wait for this hope—

READER 2: More than sentinels wait for the morning.

AUDIENCE: More than sentinels wait for the morning!

READER 2: O Israel,

READER 1: put your hope in the Lord.

AUDIENCE: Redeem us.

READER 1: He will redeem Israel,

READER 2: for the Lord has unfailing love.

READER 1: For with the Lord there is full redemption.

AUDIENCE: Then redeem us, O Lord.

READER 2: He himself will redeem Israel

READER 1: from all their sins.

AUDIENCE: We are redeemed.

22

New Things

Scriptural Base: Selected Old and New Testament Passages
Subject: Promises of Renewal, God's Blessings, New Year

Background of the Selection

Scripture has much to say about "new" things. God clearly cares about our need to feel the freshness of life. But we can look at new in two ways. We may see in that notion the idea of "brand" new, that is, never before in existence. I go to the shoe store, I buy a pair of "new" shoes. These are different from the other shoes I own. They are "brand" new. Or we may understand new as "renewed" or made over. You go to the shoe repairman and he resoles your shoes. They are now new shoes, that is, they have been remade or made over. In Scripture the great promises, as indicated by the original languages, are new in this latter sense of renewed. The new covenant is actually very old, given to our first parents. But being renewed with each generation and finally renewed in Jesus, it is "new." In this reading we review many of the new things that Bible writers mention. This reading is excellent for any occasions when renewal is emphasized-the new year, resolutions, Easter, Christmas-or when sermons stress repentance, new birth, and the like.

Ideas for Reading

Participants: READER 1, READER 2, and AUDIENCE 1, 2, 3, 4.

The READERS should be positioned at separate microphones and face the audience. They can stand next to each other or at opposite sides of the platform. The AUDIENCE needs to be divided into four fairly equal parts. You simply do this before the reading much like you would if you were leading in the singing of a round.

New Things

READER 1: Every teacher of the law—
READER 2: Who has been instructed
READER 1: about the kingdom of heaven—
READER 2: Is like the owner of a house,
READER 1: who brings out of his storeroom
READER 2: new treasures as well as old.
ALL AUDIENCES: New treasures?

READER 1: I am revitalizing everything,
READER 2: said the voice from the throne!
READER 1: Write this down,
READER 2: for these words are trustworthy and true.
ALL AUDIENCES: What is this? A new teaching?
READER 1: Yes! and with great authority!
READER 2: He even gives orders
READER 1: to evil spirits and they obey him.

READER 2: In his great mercy
READER 1: he has given us new birth
READER 2: into a living hope
READER 1: through the resurrection
READER 2: of Jesus Christ from the dead.
ALL AUDIENCES: New birth?

READER 1: He told them a parable:
READER 2: Do you pour new wine
READER 1: into old wineskins.
READER 2: If you do,
READER 1: the skins will burst,
READER 2: the wine will run out
READER 1: and the wineskins
READER 2: will be ruined.
READER 1: We don't sew patches of unshrunk cloth
READER 2: on an old garment.
READER 1: If we do, the new piece
READER 2: will pull away from the old,

READER 1: making the tear worse.
READER 2: New wine must be poured
READER 1: into new wineskins
READER 2: so we may become a new creation!
ALL AUDIENCES: May we know this new teaching?

READER 1: Christ is the mediator of a new covenant,
READER 2: that those who are called
READER 1: may receive
READER 2: the promised eternal inheritance,
READER 1: now that he has died as a ransom
READER 2: to set them free from their sins.
ALL AUDIENCES: A new covenant?
READER 1: In the same way,
READER 2: after the supper he took the cup, saying
READER 1: This cup is the new covenant in my blood
READER 2: poured out for you.
ALL AUDIENCES: A new covenant!

READER 1: At the place where Jesus was crucified,
READER 2: there was a garden.
READER 1: And in the garden a new tomb,
READER 2: in which they laid him.
READER 1: We were therefore buried with him
READER 2: through baptism into death
READER 1: so that just as Christ
READER 2: was raised from the dead,
READER 1: through the glory of the Father,
READER 2: we too may live a new life.
ALL AUDIENCES: A new life?

READER 1: He opened a new and living way
READER 2: through the curtain of his body,
AUDIENCE 1: A new way!
READER 1: Therefore,
READER 2: he is a new creation!
AUDIENCE 2: A new creation!
READER 1: The old has gone,

READER 2: the new has come!
AUDIENCE 3: The new!
READER 1: We are now created to be like God
READER 2: in righteousness and holiness.
READER 1: As believers
READER 2: you have put on the new self—
AUDIENCE 4: The new self!
READER 1: Which is being renewed in knowledge,
READER 2: in the image of its Creator.
ALL AUDIENCES: Renewed!

READER 1: A new command I give you:
READER 2: You may now love one another!
READER 1: As I have loved you,
READER 2: so you may love one another!
AUDIENCE 1: We don't need to hate anymore?
AUDIENCE 2: We don't need to criticize anymore?
AUDIENCE 3: We don't need to be judgmental anymore?
AUDIENCE 4: We don't need to act like babies anymore?
ALL AUDIENCES: We may now love—all the time??

READER 1: Neither circumcision
READER 2: nor uncircumcision
READER 1: means anything—
READER 2: Works of the law mean nothing—
READER 1: What counts is a new creation.
READER 2: His purpose was
READER 1: to create in himself
READER 2: one new person—
READER 1: To be made new
READER 2: in the attitude of your minds.
ALL AUDIENCES: A new attitude!

READER 1: In keeping with God's promise,
READER 2: we are looking forward
READER 1: to a new heaven and a new earth—
READER 2: The home of righteousness.
READER 1: Whoever has an ear,

READER 2: hear what the Spirit says!
READER 1: Whoever overcomes,
READER 2: 1 will give a new name.
ALL AUDIENCES: A new name!

READER 1: Those who overcome
READER 2: I will give the city of my God,
READER 1: the new Jerusalem,
READER 2: and I will write on them
READER 1: my new name.
ALL AUDIENCES: His new name!

READER 1: Go, stand in the temple courts,
READER 2: and tell the people the full message
READER 1: of this new life.
AUDIENCE 4: All right!
AUDIENCE 3: Amen!
AUDIENCE 2: Yes!
AUDIENCE 1: Okay!
ALL AUDIENCES: We will!

READER 1: And I saw
READER 2: a new heaven
READER 1: and a new earth,
READER 2: for the first heaven
READER 1: and the first earth
READER 2: had passed away.
AUDIENCE 1: Praise be
AUDIENCE 2: to the God
AUDIENCE 3: and Father
AUDIENCE 4: of our Lord
ALL AUDIENCES: Jesus Christ!

23

Christmas Reading

Scriptural Base: Selected Scriptural Passages
Subject: Joys of Christmas, Christ's Incarnation

Background of the Selection

The Christmas story from the Scriptures has brought inspiration to more people than any other topic in the Bible. Believers reflect on the birth of the Savior and respond in songs of adoration and praise. This reading combines the words of Advent with well-known and loved words from Christmas liturgy.

Ideas for Reading

Participants: READER 1, READER 2, READER 3, and AUDIENCE.

Place READERS in a straight line across the platform. They will read full face to the audience. The words are familiar enough to the AUDIENCE so that no practice reading is necessary. However the readers need to practice so that the combination of their reading will sound like one voice.

Christmas Reading

READER 1: Beloved in Christ,

READER 2: at this Christmas time—

READER 1: Listen—

AUDIENCE: The angels are singing!

READER 3: Let it be our care and delight

READER 1: to hear again the message of the angels—

AUDIENCE: Glory to God in the highest!

READER 2: And in heart and mind

READER 3: go to Bethlehem—

AUDIENCE: O little town of Bethlehem!

READER 2: To see this thing

READER 1: which is come to pass—

READER 3: A baby lying in a manger.

AUDIENCE: What child is this!

READER 2: We have come together

READER 1: to read the Scriptures—

AUDIENCE: There were shepherds abiding in the field!

READER 3: And to mark in our minds and hearts

READER 2: the loving purposes of the first Christmas.

AUDIENCE: O come, O come Immanuel!

READER 3: We have come together

READER 1: to read the Scriptures

READER 2: that mark out our disobedience—

AUDIENCE: All we like sheep have gone astray!

READER 3: And the glorious Redemption

READER 2: through our Lord and Savior.

AUDIENCE: There's a song in the air!

READER 1: Let us pray at this Christmas time

READER 3: for the needs of the whole world—

AUDIENCE: For peace on earth, goodwill—

READER 1: To all people—

READER 2: For goodwill among his church—

READER 3: For unity,

READER 2: for brotherhood,
READER 1: for humanhood,
READER 3: within the world,
READER 2: and especially
READER 1: within our family.

READER 3: Let us worship Jesus Christ this year—
AUDIENCE: O come to our hearts Lord Jesus!
READER 1: Let us worship Jesus Christ this year—
AUDIENCE: Thou didst leave thy throne and earthly crown!
READER 2: By remembering in his name
READER 1: the poor and helpless,
READER 3: the cold and hungry,
READER 1: the oppressed,
READER 2: the sick and those who mourn,
READER 3: the lonely,
READER 1: the unloved,
READER 2: the aged,
READER 3: the little children—
AUDIENCE: We are kings, we bear gifts to them!
READER 1: The ones who do not know the Lord Jesus,
READER 2: the ones who do not love the Lord Jesus.

READER 3: Let us rejoice
AUDIENCE: until the Son of God appears.
READER 2: He who has come
READER 3: will come again.
READER 2: He whose light shined in the tiny stable
READER 1: will shine throughout the earth.
READER 3: He whose first utterances were a baby's cry
READER 2: will become
READER 1: an invitation to eternal life.
AUDIENCE: Come, all you faithful, and enter!

READER 3: He whose first guests were a few shepherds
READER 2: will become a multitude
READER 1: that no one can number.
AUDIENCE: Glory to God in the highest!

READER 2: He who was the hope of but a few
READER 3: has become the hope of all humanity!
READER 2: The swaddling clothes
READER 1: have become a royal robe!
READER 3: The manger
READER 2: has became a throne
AUDIENCE: in David's royal city!
READER 1: The stable
READER 3: has become our hearts
READER 2: in which the Savior lives.
AUDIENCE: Even so come Lord Jesus!
READER 1: Even so come again Jesus—
READER 2: Come again and be our Lord.

24

Thankfulness

Scriptural Base: The Lord's Supper
Subject: Communion, Gratitude

Background of the Selection

In Christian community the Lord's Supper embodies the story of salvation and our response to it. Our Lord acted his part in the salvation of humanity, and demonstrated our part as well. The Lord's Supper renews our commitment to serve each time we actively celebrate it. Jesus said the last supper was to be with us until He would eat with us in the kingdom! In this reading we look at service to others in the context of our own lives.

Ideas for Reading

Participants: READER 1, READER 2, and AUDIENCE.

Place READERS at separate microphones facing the audience. The food recipe section should be read rather rapidly compared to the other parts of the reading. The recipe's importance is in its connection with everyday life and not in the details of the ingredients. (The recipe is a *bona fide* one!) The AUDIENCE represents humanity that wants to get on with life, in this case eating, but is led to the source of all blessings. The reading leads the congregation to blend the physical needs to the spiritual needs as so well articulated in the story of the Lord's Supper. Advise the AUDIENCE to read individually with feeling and not to be concerned with uniform response.

Thankfulness

READER 1: One package dry yeast
READER 2: or one cake compressed yeast.
READER 1: One fourth cup water,
READER 2: two cups of milk scalded.
READER 1: Two tablespoons of sugar,
READER 2: six teaspoons of salt,
READER 1: one tablespoon of shortening,
READER 2: six and one half cups
READER 1: of sifted enriched flour.
READER 2: Then—soften and add,
READER 1: turn and knead,
READER 2: shape and place,
READER 1: punch and divide,
READER 2: bake and serve.
AUDIENCE: Give thanks and then eat!

READER 1: But first—
READER 2: How many loaves do you have?
AUDIENCE: Seven.
READER 1: Then Jesus took
READER 2: the seven loaves
READER 1: divided and served
AUDIENCE: But first gave thanks—
READER 2: So that all could eat!

READER 1: Two tablespoons salt,
READER 2: one half cup milk,
READER 1: two and one half halibut steaks,
READER 2: one and one half cups
READER 1: slightly crushed corn flakes,
READER 2: two tablespoons melted butter
READER 1: or margarine.
READER 2: Dissolve and dip,
READER 1: pour and shake,
READER 2: bake and serve—
AUDIENCE: Give thanks and eat.

READER 2: But first—
READER 1: How many fish do you have?
AUDIENCE: Two small ones.
READER 1: Then Jesus took
READER 2: the two small fish
READER 1: divided and served—
AUDIENCE: But first gave thanks—
READER 2: So that all could eat!

READER 1: On the same night that He was betrayed
READER 2: Jesus took the bread,
READER 1: broke it—
AUDIENCE: And gave thanks.

READER 1: On the same night that He was betrayed
READER 2: Jesus took the wine,
READER 1: poured it—
AUDIENCE: And gave thanks.

READER 2: On that very same night that He was betrayed
READER 1: He gave his body
AUDIENCE: so that *all* could live.
READER 1: On that very same night
READER 2: he gave his blood
AUDIENCE: so that all could be forgiven.
READER 2: To which we say in gratitude—
AUDIENCE: Thank you Lord!

READER 1: Three words in due season,
READER 2: one and one half visits to the sick
READER 1: three meals to the hungry,
READER 2: two long sleeve shirts from your back
READER 1: to the shirtless,
READER 2: five, one-half hour visits to prisoners
READER 1: Then—
READER 2: pray and visit,
READER 1: sing and talk,

READER 2: cry and laugh,
READER 1: empathize and sympathize
AUDIENCE: and give thanks and live—
READER 2: For now you have worshiped God!

READER 1: I will tell you the truth:
READER 2: whatever you did
READER 1: for one of the least of these
READER 2: you did for me.
READER 1: Go away to eternal life!

READER 2: God takes our
AUDIENCE: seven loaves.
READER 1: God takes our
AUDIENCE: two fishes
ALL READERS: and give thanks.
READER 1: We take his blood.
READER 2: We take his body.
AUDIENCE: We become His sons and daughters.
ALL: Amen.

25

The Cost of Following Jesus

Scriptural Base: Matthew 8:18–22
Subject: Discipleship

Background of the Selection

Self-sacrifice characterized Jesus' life. He made it abundantly clear that He was not of this world nor did He follow after the things of this world. At first his disciples followed Him because they wanted to occupy honored places in His new government. But they soon learned that following Jesus involves *costly grace*. In our reading Jesus again stresses that following Him has its cost and its reward.

Ideas for Reading

Participants: READER 1, READER 2, and AUDIENCE.

In this reading the AUDIENCE responds to the words of Jesus concerning the cost of following Him. READERS read the words of Jesus with the AUDIENCE responding but not really listening to the words. Separate the READERS on the platform.

The Cost of Following Jesus

READER 1: There is a cost—
READER 2: A price to pay—
READER 1: For whatever is done
READER 2: or whomever we follow.
READER 1: The Son of Man—
AUDIENCE: I will follow Him.
READER 2: Has no place to rest.

READER 1: Foxes have holes,
READER 2: birds haves nests.
READER 1: Follow me.
AUDIENCE: I will follow Him—
READER 2: But—
AUDIENCE: Yes, but first let me—
READER 1: But first let me bury my father?
READER 2: Dead can bury the dead,
READER 1: but only life can proclaim the kingdom.

READER 2: Follow me—
AUDIENCE: Yes, but first let me—
READER 1: But first let me go back.
READER 2: and say good-bye to my family?
READER 1: No one who puts
READER 2: his hand to the plough
READER 1: and looks back
READER 2: is fit for service
READER 1: in the kingdom.
AUDIENCE: But what of my dead father—
READER 2: And your family?

READER 1: Following is *doing*
READER 2: not *excusing.*
READER 1: Following is *proclaiming*
READER 2: not *procrastinating,*
READER 1: Seek first the kingdom,
READER 2: and the needs

READER 1: of your family
READER 2: will be cared for.
AUDIENCE: Yes—but—well—
READER 1: No buts or wells,
READER 2: just commitment
READER 1: to the kingdom of God.

26

The Beatitudes

Scriptural Base. Matthew 5
Subject: God's Blessings, Spirituality

Background of the Selection

Perhaps the greatest sermon in the Bible is the "Sermon on the Mount."

In the beginning of this sermon we have the blessings of God or "the beatitudes." Here Jesus gives spiritual responses to the joys and tragedies of the human experience. Many of the spiritual leaders of Jesus' time begrudgingly allowed for joys in life because they attributed the tragedies of life to personal sin. Rather than get too excited about life we should be constantly be reminded of its dark side, they taught. Jesus shows that through sadness and triumph God is ever present in the believer's life. Through these experiences believers show others how to respond as a follower of Christ. As we develop a relationship with Christ we see God in the experiences of this life.

Ideas for Reading

Participants: READER 1, READER 2, and AUDIENCE.

The AUDIENCE is cast as one of the disciples of Jesus responding to the sermon. READER I and READER 2 carry the story line and thus are cast as Jesus as he teaches the people on the mountainside. Encourage the READERS to read in a conversational tone, empathetic to the responses of the AUDIENCE. The AUDIENCE needs to respond with questioning voices. Remind the AUDIENCE to note the punctuation marks, for example encourage a voice of dismay when they read the line, "But what am I for?"

The Beatitudes

READER 1: All of you are the salt of the earth.
READER 2: If salt loses its saltiness,
READER 1: it is useless,
READER 2: except
READER 1: to be thrown out and walked on by people.
READER 2: You are salt.
READER 1: All of you are the salt of the earth.
AUDIENCE: I am salt?
READER 1: You are the salt.
READER 2: You are also the light of the earth.
AUDIENCE: Salt and light?

READER 2: As a city on a hill
READER 1: you can't be hid.
READER 2: Salt tastes,
READER 1: light shines,
READER 2: as cities are seen in the darkness.
AUDIENCE: But what am I for?
READER 1: To give light,
READER 2: to give flavor.

AUDIENCE: To be seen?
READER 1: Yes! By everyone!
READER 2: Your light shines,
READER 1: as your good deeds are felt.
READER 2: People praise your Father in heaven
READER 1: as they are filled
READER 2: and satisfied.

AUDIENCE: So what do I have to do?
READER 1: Just be salt and light.
READER 2: People will see
READER 1: and praise your Father in heaven
READER 1: if you just allow the salt do its salting
READER 2: and let the light do its shining!

AUDIENCE: I don't feel worthy.
READER 2: That's okay—the kingdom of heaven is still yours.
READER 1: Those who feel the need will want heaven.
AUDIENCE: Sometimes I'm very sad.
READER 1: You will be comforted.
READER 2: True joy sometimes comes
READER 1: in the wake of sadness.

AUDIENCE: I want to be good.
READER 2: Your hunger and thirst for righteousness
READER 1: will be satisfied.
READER 2: And since you are merciful
READER 1: you will be shown mercy.
AUDIENCE: Will I ever see God!
READER 2: You will,
READER 1: and it will purify your heart.
READER 2: Not only will you see God
READER 1: you can now become his Son and Daughter
READER 2: by becoming a peacemaker.

AUDIENCE: I feel persecuted at times.
READER 1: Yours is the kingdom of heaven!
AUDIENCE: I have been insulted.
READER 2: I'm sure many have said
READER 1: all kinds of evil against you,
READER 2: falsely, of course.
AUDIENCE: What then?
READER 1: Rejoice.
READER 2: Rejoice.
AUDIENCE: But, why?

READER 2: You live in the tradition
READER 1: of the world's great teacher.
READER 2: Great is your reward in heaven.
READER 1: Sometimes through your weakness
READER 1: God will be seen:
READER 2: the poor in spirit,
READER 1: the sad,

READER 2: the meek.

READER 1: The light and flavor of heaven will show through you:

READER 2: the persecuted.

READER 1: the merciful,

READER 2: the pure,

READER 1: the peacemakers.

AUDIENCE: Then I am this salt and light!

READER 1: You are the salt in the entire world,

READER 2: and the light for all people to see God.

READER 1: As the father has sent Jesus to this world

READER 2: so he sends you.

27

The Wise and Foolish Men

Scriptural Base: Matthew 7
Subject: Grounding Your Faith in God, Doing God's Will

Background of the Selection

Bible students usually interpret Christ be the rock in this parable. We have good reasons to perceive of Christ as the Rock of our salvation. But Jesus is also the Word (John 1:1–3). In this passage we see the importance of grounding our faith in Jesus as the Word of God. Such grounding is like building your life on a rock. We emphasize here that believers need to listen and act on Jesus as their Word. Unless Jesus' mentoring changes lives what have we got? In ignoring the Word we will end up like the foolish man whose house is swept away in the storm.

Ideas for Reading

Participants: READER 1, READER 2, AUDIENCE 1 and AUDIENCE 2.

The AUDIENCE is divided into two equal parts. AUDIENCE 1 is cast as the wise man, AUDIENCE 2 as the foolish man. Both AUDIENCES need to read with optimism in an upbeat manner, except the last AUDIENCE 2 line, "My house is ruined." Point out to AUDIENCE 2 to read this line with surprise as though they were oblivious to the preceding words. The last five lines of the reading should be read quite slowly, emphasizing the fact that hearing and listening to Jesus means following Jesus.

The Wise and Foolish Men

READER 1: Jesus told a very interesting story.
READER 2: As is often the case
READER 1: people remember the story
READER 2: but not always the meaning of the story.
READER 1: The parable of the wise builder
READER 2: and the foolish builder
READER 1: is just such a story.

READER 2: Jesus said,
READER 1: Anyone who hears my words
AUDIENCE 1: Speak Lord.
READER 1: And puts them into practice…
AUDIENCE 1: I will do as you say!
READER 2: Is like a wise man.
AUDIENCE 1: I will build a house.
READER 1: When you build
READER 2: build on a rock.
AUDIENCE 1: I will.

READER 1: And so he did.
READER 2: When the rains came,
READER 1: as they always do,
READER 2: the streams began to rise,
READER 1: and the wind began to blow,
READER 2: and beat against the house.
AUDIENCE 1: My house is still standing!
READER 1: Your house is still standing
READER 2: because you heard and did the words of Jesus
READER 1: And Jesus said to another man,
READER 2: Those who hear my words
AUDIENCE 2: Speak Lord!
READER 1: And don't put them into practice
READER 2: Are like a foolish man.
AUDIENCE 2: I will build a house.
READER 1: When you build

READER 2: secure your house to a rock.
AUDIENCE 2: I will!

READER 1: But he didn't!
READER 2: He built his house on sand.
READER 1: When it began to rain
READER 2: As it always does,
READER 2: The streams began to rise,
READER 1: And the winds began to blow,
READER 2: and they beat against the house,
AUDIENCE 2: My house is ruined!
READER 1: And it actually fell flat.
READERS 1, 2: Crash!

READER 1: And it did fall
READER 2: because he heard the words
READER 1: but didn't do the words.
READER 2: Anyone who hears my words
READER 1: and puts them into practice is wise!

28

Healings

Scriptural Base: Matthew 9
Subject: Miracles, Power of Christ, Spiritual and Physical Healing, Faith

Background of the Selection

For much of Jesus' ministry crowds huddled about him trying to get something from him. Some tried to catch him uttering blasphemous statements, some gathered spiritual strength, and some wanted to be entertained. This passage tells of people who wanted healing. Two people approached Jesus in two different ways. One confronted him face to face in faith while the other just wanted to touch his garment, also in faith. Neither were disappointed in their trust in Jesus! Both were healed.

Ideas for Reading

Participants: JESUS, READER 1, READER 2, AUDIENCE 1, and AUDIENCE 2.

Divide the AUDIENCE into two groups. We suggest that you briefly discuss the role of two groups. AUDIENCE 1 plays the ruler that speaks directly to Jesus. The lines of AUDIENCE 1 should be spoken in confidence. AUDIENCE 2 plays the woman who has been sick for 12 years. Her lines are spoken quietly but with confidence. AUDIENCES 1 and 2 carry the story line and should be read with expression.

Healings

READER 1: While Jesus was teaching
READER 2: a ruler
READER 1: and a woman
READER 2: came to him.
READER 1: The ruler knelt in front of him and said,
AUDIENCE 1: My daughter has just died.
READER 2: And Jesus got up
AUDIENCE 1: Please come—
READER 1: And he went with him.

AUDIENCE 1: Put your hand on her, and she will be healed.
READER 1: Just then the woman—
READER 2: Who had bled for twelve years—
READER 1: Came up behind him and thought:
AUDIENCE 2: If I could only touch his cloak—
READER 2: She pushed her way through the crowd and thought,
AUDIENCE 2: I will be healed.

READER 1: As she touched the cloak Jesus turned and saw her.
JESUS: Take heart, daughter, your faith has healed you.
READER 2: And the woman was healed from that moment.
AUDIENCE 2: 1 am healed!

AUDIENCE 1: Master, my child is still dead!
READER 1: Later that day when Jesus entered the ruler's house
READER 2: he saw the flute players and the noisy crowd.
JESUS: Go away.
READER 1: They laughed at him.
JESUS: The girl is not dead, she's asleep.
READER 1: Again they laughed at him.

READER 2: But after the crowd had been put outside,
READER 1: he went in and took the girl by the hand.
JESUS: Arise!
READER 2: And she got up.
READER 1: And so it was

READER 2: that the good news of this event
READER 1: spread throughout all
READER 2: that region—
READER 1: The good news of healing—this was the good news—
READER 2: that life was in the land.
AUDIENCE 1: Jesus has healed my daughter.
AUDIENCE 2: Jesus has healed me.

29

The Sower

Scriptural Base: Matthew 13
Subject: Miracles, Power of Christ

Background of the Selection

Jesus had the great ability to tell stories that related to the people's daily existence. In the parable of the sower he dealt with basic life. One can imagine a farmer casting seeds while Jesus spoke. Of course everyone, even to the children, could relate to this farmer's successes and failures with the seeds. No story in Scripture conveys better that this one that life results from contact with the kingdom of God. This reading intertwines the successes and failure in the preaching of the gospel throughout the New Testament.

Ideas for Reading

Participants: READER 1, READER 2, READER 3, and AUDIENCE.

The AUDIENCE plays a thoughtful disciple who is absorbed in the teaching of the parable. Place READERS 1, 2, and 3 an equal distance apart and use separate microphones if possible. Pause after the AUDIENCE line, "Like the seed on the good soil." The READERS read the ending with intensity and feeling.

The Sower

READER 1: Through the centuries—
READER 2: People have said and thought—
AUDIENCE: Teach us of the kingdom!

READER 3: A farmer went out to plant—
READER 1: a farmer who was not always careful
READER 2: where he threw the seeds.
AUDIENCE: Sooooo—

READER 3: Some fell on the path;
READER 1: but before seeds could grow—
READER 2: or be picked up by the farmer—
READER 3: the birds came and ate the seeds.
AUDIENCE: Like pearls before swine?

READER 1: Yes, even so, the farmer continued his careless sowing
READER 2: and some fell on the rocks
READER 1: where some soil gave it nourishment.
AUDIENCE: Then what?
READER 1: The seed sprouted.
READER 2: But—
READER 3: But the sun came out and scorched the plants.
AUDIENCE: As Judas went out and hung himself?

READER 1: Yes, but the careless farmer
READER 2: continued sowing his seeds
READER 3: and some fell among jagged thorns.
READER 2: These seeds sprouted and grew
AUDIENCE: but—so did the thorns,
READER 3: and they choked out the little plants.
AUDIENCE: As Ananias lied and died?

READER 1: Yes, and the persistent—
READER 3: But "careless" farmer threw some seeds
READER 2: that fell in good soil
READER 3: where they produced a healthy crop.

AUDIENCE: As the Lord added to their number daily?
READER 1: Yes, a hundred
READER 2: sixty,
READER 3: or thirty times,
AUDIENCE: 3000 were baptized!

READER 1: Listen to my words of the kingdom
READER 2: or the words will be lost.
AUDIENCE: Like seeds on the path!
READER 1: Yes—listen to my words of the kingdom!
READER 3: Put away worries and deceitfulness
READER 1: or my words will be lost.
AUDIENCE: Like seeds among thorns!
READER 1: Listen to my words of the kingdom
READER 3: or when persecution and trouble come
READER 1: the words will be lost—
AUDIENCE: Like the seeds on rocks!

READER 1: Yes—listen to my words of the kingdom
READER 3: and you will grow unto eternal life.
AUDIENCE: Like the seed on the good soil.

READER 1: This is the story
READER 3: of how people respond
READER 2: to the words of eternal life.
READER 1: It is the story
READER 2: of a "careless" farmer
READER 3: who sows seeds everywhere
READER 1: so that some will sprout.
READER 2: It is the story
READER 3: of a loving God
READER 2: who gives sunshine and rain
READER 1: to the good and the bad
READER 2: so that his Word can find a place
ALL READERS: in all our hearts!

30

The Tenants

Scriptural Base: Matthew 21
Subject: Christian responsibility, Accountability, God's love

Background of the Selection

The parable of the tenants gives a sad commentary of some people's response to the Gospel story. Some would rather have position and money than be fair and honest with others. Perhaps the parable tells us more about the owner than the tenants. It shows how God will do anything to communicate his love to us. But ultimately a day of accountability arrives. The story relates how all will stand before the judgment seat of God. And at that time no one will say that God is unfair.

Ideas for Reading

Participants: READER 1, READER 2, and AUDIENCE.

In this Interactive Reading the AUDIENCE plays the owner of the field and reflects the thoughts of God. Encourage the AUDIENCE to read with feeling as they find that all efforts to be fair are met with scorn and death. The READERS 1 and 2 should read their lines in a very probing manner.

The Tenants

READER 1: You have just purchased
READER 2: a piece of property.
READER 1: What would you like to do with it?
AUDIENCE: Plant a vineyard on it.
READER 1: Anything else?
AUDIENCE: Put a wall around it.
READER 2: What about building a watchtower?
AUDIENCE: Yes, a watchtower.
READER 1: Is that all? A Winepress?
AUDIENCE: I need a winepress.

READER 2: Now you are going to be out of town.
READER 1: Who's going to care of the vineyard?
AUDIENCE: I'll hire some farmers.
READER 2: And that is indeed what happened.

READER 1: But as the harvest approached,
READER 2: Sir—
READER 1: You sent how many servants to collect rent?
AUDIENCE: Three, why?
READER 1: Well,
READER 2: one was beaten.
AUDIENCE: On my land?
READER 1: One was stoned
READER 2: and one was killed.
AUDIENCE: All in my vineyard?
READER 1: Yes, what now?
AUDIENCE: Hire more farmers.
READER 1: And that's what he did.

READER 2: He sent more farmers than before with these results—
READER 1: Sir, you sent more farmers.
AUDIENCE: Yes.
READER 2: The tenants beat one.
AUDIENCE: Not again!
READER 2: Stoned two,

READER 1: and killed three.

AUDIENCE: All on my land?

READER 2: Now what do you want to do?

AUDIENCE: Only one thing left—

READER 1: And what is that?

AUDIENCE: *(sigh)* I'll send my own son!

READER 2: Your only son?

AUDIENCE: Yes, they will respect him.

READER 1: You want to send your only son?

AUDIENCE: I'll send my only son.

READER 2: And the landowner did just that

READER 1: but with these results.

READER 2: Sir, your only son is dead.

AUDIENCE: Dead?

READER 1: The tenants killed him.

AUDIENCE: Why? They are renters!

READER 2: When the tenants saw your only son

READER 1: they said,

READER 2: this is the heir.

READER 1: Come and let us kill him!

AUDIENCE: My son is the heir.

READER 2: The tenants took your only son,

READER 1: threw him out of the vineyard—

AUDIENCE: But I own it!

READER 1: and killed him.

READER 2: And they took the profits from the vineyard

READER 1: in addition to their salary.

AUDIENCE: I am going to the vineyard myself!

READER 1: You are going yourself.

READER 2: What are you going to do?

AUDIENCE: Bring a wretched end to them.

READER 1: All of those wretches?

AUDIENCE: Yes.

READER 1: Then?

AUDIENCE: Rent it out again.

READER 2: Again?
AUDIENCE: To those who will pay rent!

READER 1: So the kingdom of heaven
READER 2: is like a land owner,
READER 1: who only expects the rent to be paid,
READER 2: and the tenants to respect his only Son.

31

Two Sons

Scriptural Base: Matthew 21
Subject: Works of Faith, Loyalty, Honesty

Background of the Selection

Jesus continually dealt with religious leaders who talked a good line but seldom delivered the goods. The two sons represent the human experience, saying yes but not following through with their actions. The religious leaders of Jesus' day often said politically correct things but either did nothing or did the very opposite. In this story Jesus draws a line between the genuine and the counterfeit—the *wanabees* and the *believers*.

Ideas for Reading

Participants: READER 1, READER 2, and AUDIENCE.

The AUDIENCE is divided into two parts. Make the AUDIENCE 1 and AUDIENCE 2 aware of their role in this story so that they can act the part with their voices. AUDIENCE 1 plays the part of the son who eventually does the work, while AUDIENCE 2 plays the part of the son who says but does not. The READERS carry the story line including the part of the Father. Again the READERS need to read with emphasis as needed.

Two Sons

READER 2: Jesus asked a simple question,
READER 1: about a very simple story.
READER 2: Now what do you think?

READER 1: A man
READER 2: had two sons and a vineyard,
READER 1: with plenty of work to do in it.
READER 2: He said
READER 1: to son number one—
READER 2: Go!
AUDIENCE 1: No!
READER 1: Work in my field.
AUDIENCE 1: I won't go!
READER 1: Son—go and work in my field today.
AUDIENCE 1: I won't go.
AUDIENCE 2: Shame on him.

READER 2: But later
READER 1: son number one
READER 2: changed his mind
READER 1: and went and did the work in the vineyard.
AUDIENCE 2: Now that's better.

READER 2: Then to son number two
READER 1: the man said,
READER 2: Go and work in my field.
AUDIENCE 1: I can use the help!
READER 2: Go and work in my field today.
AUDIENCE 2: Oh yes, I'll go.
READER 1: But
READER 2: even though son number two said,
AUDIENCE 2: Oh yes, I'll go—
READER 2: He never showed up!
AUDIENCE 1: Where is my brother?

READER 1: Now which of the two
READER 2: did the will of his father?
READER 1: The son who said,
AUDIENCE 1: I won't go—
READER 2: But later did?
READER 1: Or—
READER 2: The son who said,
AUDIENCE 2: Oh yes, I will go,
READER 2: but never showed up?
READER 1: Which did the will of the father?
AUDIENCES 1, 2: The first son!

READER 1: I'm going to tell you something—
READER 2: The truth of matter is this—
READER 1: Talking is not doing.
READER 2: Believing is not doing.

READER 1: The kingdom of Heaven is
READER 2: is made up of people
READER 1: who hear the words of Jesus
READER 1, 2: and act upon them.

32

The Wedding Garment

Scriptural Base: Matthew 21
Subject: Being ready, Concern for others, Putting God first

Background of the Selection

Three events in life bring people together like no other: births, weddings, and deaths. In Jesus' day to ignore a wedding invitation would be impolite in the first place and then to attend without being properly dressed would add insult to injury. This parable tells the story of a man's total disregard of joys of others in the wedding. It gives a graphic description of people whose values are misplaced and of the value of God's gift to humankind.

Ideas for Reading

Participants: READER 1, READER 2, READER 3, AUDIENCE 1 and AUDIENCE 2.

The AUDIENCE plays the person who continually refuses the invitation and the one that finally comes to the wedding reception but attends improperly dressed. The AUDIENCE should read with disdain throughout the reading. The three READERS assume the roles of storyteller and king.

The Wedding Garment

READER 1: This story tells about heaven,
READER 2: a king, and a wedding garment.
READER 3: This story tells
READER 1: about servants and a banquet,
READER 3: oxen and cattle,
READER 1: business and killing,
READER 2: good and bad,
READER 3: invitations and choices,
READER 1: and a wedding hall ready for the guests.

READER 2: The kingdom of heaven
READER 1: is like a king preparing
READER 3: a wedding banquet for his son.
READER 2: Go to all those who are invited.
READER 1: Tell them to come to the banquet!
READER 3: Come to the banquet.
AUDIENCE 1: No, we won't!

READER 3: But the king wanted guests
READER 1: for the wedding banquet.
READER 2: So—
READER 1: He sent more servants
READER 2: to tell them to come to the prepared dinner.
READER 3: Come to the wedding banquet.
AUDIENCE 1: No, we still won't!

READER 1: But the ox is ready—
AUDIENCE 1: No!
READER 3: The fattened cattle have been—
AUDIENCE 1: No!
READER 1: Come to the wedding banquet—
AUDIENCE 1: No, we won't!
READER 1: And to make sure the king
READER 2: knew that NO meant NO,
READER 3: they seized his servants,
READER 1: mistreated them,

READER 3: and killed them.
AUDIENCE 1: We have business to care for!

READER 1: But the king was determined to have guests at the wedding feast.
READER 2: So—
READER 3: He told some of his other servants—
READER 1: Go to the street corners,
READER 2: and the avenues,
READER 1: and the lanes,
READER 3: and invite everyone to attend the feast for my son.
READER 2: And they took the message to the good and bad alike.
READER 3: Won't you come to the wedding banquet!
AUDIENCE 2: Yes, we will! We will be glad to!!

READER 3: The wedding hall
READER 2: was finally filled with guests all dressed in wedding garments—
READER 1: Well—almost everyone.
READER 2: It was announced that someone did not have a wedding garment on!
AUDIENCE 2: Is it I Lord?
READER 3: How did you get in here
READER 2: without wearing a wedding garment?
AUDIENCE 2: Well, I just—
READER 1: *(pause)* Tie him up!
AUDIENCE 2: But, I just thought—
READER 1: Well—but, I just thought nothing—
READER 3: Tie him hand and foot.
READER 2: Throw him outside
READER 3: for he is no better
READER 2: than those who refused to come.

READER 1: The kingdom of heaven is about
READER 3: listening and accepting,
READER 2: coming and doing,
READER 3: about being invited and choosing,
READER 1: about being accepted and willfully obeying.
AUDIENCES 1, 2: We all are invited, but few choose.

33

The Least of These

Scriptural Base: Matthew 25
Subject: Christian responsibility, True religion

Background of the Selection

Throughout his ministry, Jesus identified with the less fortunate and the needy. While the Jews of his day generally thought of the poor and sick as those cursed of God, Jesus insisted that in helping these classes we are directly helping him. Such an unusual notion has caused centuries of contemplation. We still have difficulty seeing God in the empty stomach, the diseases of people, the jail cells of murderers. This reading emphasizes the well-known statement of Jesus, "In that you have done it unto the least of these you have done it unto me."

Ideas for Reading

Participants: READER 1, READER 2, JESUS, and AUDIENCE.

In this reading the AUDIENCE plays a follower of Jesus who is unaware that in helping the needy of society (s)he is dealing directly with Jesus. The AUDIENCE should respond with incredulity throughout the reading. JESUS should be positioned separate and between the two READERS. The three should be as far apart as possible on the platform.

The Least of These

READER 1: When the Son of Man returns
READER 2: He will arrive in all his glory.
READER 1: He will return with his angels.
READER 2: He will arrive on His heavenly throne.

READER 1: When the King returns—
READER 2: And he will return!
READER 1: He will say these words,
JESUS: Gather around, you who are blessed by the Father.
AUDIENCE: You mean us?

JESUS: Here, take your inheritance, the kingdom of heaven.
AUDIENCE: But—but why us?
JESUS: I was hungry and you gave me something to eat.
AUDIENCE: We have never seen you hungry.
JESUS: I was thirsty and you have me something to drink.
AUDIENCE: We did?
JESUS: I was a stranger and you invited me in.
AUDIENCE: In our homes?
JESUS: I was sick and you looked after me.
AUDIENCE: You were sick?
JESUS: I was in prison and you came to visit me.
AUDIENCE: You were in prison?

READER 1: Then when the Son of Man goes back to heaven
READER 2: He will return with all of his glory.
READER 1: He will return with his angels.
READER 2: He will return to His heavenly throne.
READER 1: When the King returns to heaven—
READER 2: And he will return!

READER 1: He will return with those—
JESUS: Those who fed me, who clothed me, who nursed me, who visited me, who looked after me, who loved me.
AUDIENCE: When was all this?
JESUS: By helping the least of humanity—you helped me!

READER 1: And so it will be that the King will return to heaven

READER 2: with those who cared for

READER 1: The homeless.

READER 2: The housebound.

READER 1: The prisoners.

READER 2: The latch-key kids—

READER 1: Any kids—

READER 2: The bereaved.

READER 1: The sick.

READER 2: The lonely.

READER 1: The tired.

READER 2: The students.

JESUS: If you have done it unto the least of these, you have done it unto me.

34

The Talents

Scriptural Base: Matthew 25
Subject: Responsibility, Gifts, God's Goodness

Background of the Selection

Throughout Scripture salvation comes from God as a gift, pure and simple. The gift makes us responsible for our actions and the use of our God-given abilities. The parable of the talents makes it clear that whatever we have we must either use or lose. The story provides a prescription for growth as a person.

Ideas for Reading

Participants: READER 1, READER 2, and AUDIENCE.

The AUDIENCE plays a businessman applying good business principles to the situation. The two READERS are in conversation with this businessman.

The Talents

READER 1: A man was going on a journey.
READER 2: Tell me, what do you think?
READER 1: The man was quite rich, had an extra eight talents of money,
READER 2: and was going on a long trip.
READER 1: What should he do with this money?
AUDIENCE: Loan it out!
READER 1: To his three servants?
AUDIENCE: Why not?
READER 2: How should he divide it?
READER 1: Evenly.
AUDIENCE: No.
READER 2: How then?
AUDIENCE: According to their ability.

READER 1: So to the one with the most ability—
AUDIENCE: Give five talents.
READER 2: And to the next smartest—
AUDIENCE: Give two talents.
READER 1: And to the third servant—
AUDIENCE: Give him the one talent left.

READER 1: What should the servants do with the money?
AUDIENCE: Invest it!
READER 2: And so they did—
READER 1: well most of them did.
READER 2: The five-talent person
READER 1: ended up with ten talents.
READER 2: The two-talent person
READER 1: ended up with four talents.
READER 2: The one-talent person
READER 1: ended up with one talent.
AUDIENCE: He didn't invest, did he?
READER 2: No, he didn't.
READER 1: He hid it in the ground!
AUDIENCE: In the ground?!

READER 2: What do you think the rich man
READER 1: will say to each servant
READER 2: when he comes home to collect on his loan?
READER 1: To the five-talent man
READER 2: who brings in ten talents—
READER 1: What do you think the rich man will say to him?
AUDIENCE: **Well done, good and faithful servant!**
READER 1: What will he say to the two-talent man
READER 2: who brings in four talents—
AUDIENCE: **Well done!**
READER 1: For men who double their talents
READER 2: how would the rich man reward them—
AUDIENCE: **Put them in charge.**
READER 1: Anything else?
AUDIENCE: **Share the Master's happiness!**

READER 1: Now the one-talent man
READER 2: came back with the same one talent.
READER 1: With
READER 2: lots of dirt on it from the ground
READER 1: and with—
READER 2: Lots of excuses,
READER 1: such as—
READER 1: The master reaps where he doesn't sow.

READER 2: Now, what would you call such a man?
AUDIENCE: **Wicked, lazy and worthless.**
READER 2: Wicked, lazy and worthless?
AUDIENCE: **He didn't invest.**
READER 1: What would you do, with him?
AUDIENCE: **Take his talents from him,**
READER 2: and
AUDIENCE: **BURN HIM!**

READER 1: For everyone who has, will be given more.
READER 2: Whoever does not use will lose.

READER 1: If you live your life unto yourself
READER 2: you will die unto yourself.
READERS 1, 2: For of such is the kingdom of heaven.

35

Greatness

Scriptural Base: Mark 10
Subject: Humility, Greatness, Pride

Background of the Selection

Even though the disciples had been with Jesus a long time they still did not understand his mission to this world or the true character of God. Servants were necessary to the Jewish economy but certainly not considered first class spiritual citizens. This particular story had great significance to the disciples. Greatness has special meaning for the believer. In this reading James and John have a chance to dialogue on that special meaning.

Ideas for Reading

Participants: READER 1, READER 2, JESUS, AUDIENCE 1 and AUDIENCE 2.

The AUDIENCE is divided into two parts. AUDIENCE 1 is cast as John and AUDIENCE 2 is cast as James. Mention to the audience that James and John were sons of thunder, and they need to speak with forceful and confident voices. READERS 1 and 2 should be separated from each other with Jesus standing between and in front of them. JESUS reads as if he is speaking directly to the disciples.

Greatness

READER 1: James and John,
READER 2: the sons of Zebedee,
READER 1: came to Jesus with this question,
AUDIENCE 1: Teacher, will you do us a favor?

JESUS: What do you want me to do for you?
AUDIENCE 2: Let us sit by you on your throne.

JESUS: You don't know what you are asking.
AUDIENCE 1: Yes, but why?
JESUS: Can you drink the cup I drink?
AUDIENCE 2: I can!
JESUS: Or be baptized with the baptism I am baptized with?
AUDIENCE 1: I can!

JESUS: You will drink the cup I drink, and be baptized with the baptism I am baptized with, but to sit at my right or left hand is not for me to grant. These places belong to those for whom they have been prepared.

READER 1: When the other ten disciples heard about this
READER 2: they were mad at James and John.
READER 1: Jesus called them together and said,
JESUS: You know that those who are regarded as rulers of the Gentiles lord it over them?
AUDIENCE 2: Yes.
JESUS: And their high officials exercise authority over them.

AUDIENCE 1: We would like to be great.
JESUS: To be great you must become a servant.
AUDIENCE 1, 2: A servant!

JESUS: To be first you must be slave of all. I did not come to be served. I came to serve, and to give my life as a ransom.

READER 2: All of these words were not lost on James and John
READER 1: and they were baptized with the baptism of Christ.

READER 2: On the island of Patmos John lived out his last days.
READER 1: And by the sword James meet his death as one of the first Christian martyrs.

36

Helping Those In Need

Scriptural Base: Luke 10
Subject: Brotherhood

Background of the Selection

The story of the Good Samaritan, one of the best known of Jesus' parables, has its setting in the daily life of the Israelites. The story rebukes the lawyer who asks Jesus the question. In so doing Jesus rebuked the whole nation because in this story an outsider acts like a believer should. The story packs as much of a force today as it did 2000 years ago.

Ideas for Reading

Participants: READER 1, READER 2, JESUS, and AUDIENCE.

The AUDIENCE is cast as the lawyer, who appears to be an honest seeker of truth. This should be reflected in the AUDIENCE'S tone of voice. Place JESUS downstage center, with the two READERS on either side of the platform.

Helping Those In Need

READER 1: On one occasion a lawyer stood up to test Jesus.
AUDIENCE: Teacher—
READER 2: Then he asked this question,
AUDIENCE: What must I do to inherit eternal life?

JESUS: What is written in the Law?
AUDIENCE: Love the Lord your God.
JESUS: You say well.

READER 1: The lawyer went on to say that this love was
READER 2: involved all of the soul and heart,
READER 1: involved all of one's strength,
READER 2: involved all of the mind.

JESUS: And what else do you read?
AUDIENCE: Love your neighbor as yourself.
JESUS: You have answered correctly, do this and you will live.

READER 1: But the lawyer wanted to justify himself,
READER 2: so he asked Jesus,
AUDIENCE: Who is my neighbor?

READER 1: Jesus, instead of just answering—
JESUS: A neighbor is anyone in need,
READER 2: told this story.

JESUS: A man was going down from Jerusalem to Jericho.
READER 1: And he fell into the hands of robbers.
READER 2: They stripped him.
READER 1: They beat him.
READER 2: They left him for dead.
READER 1: A priest,
READER 2: going down the same road,
READER 1: saw the man
JESUS: and passed by on the other side.
READER 2: A Levite,

READER 1: going down the same road
READER 2: saw the same wounded man.
JESUS: He did just as the priest did—passed by on the other side.

READER 1: A Samaritan,
READER 2: going down the same road
READER 1: saw the man.
JESUS: The Samaritan man took pity on him and stopped.
READER 2: He bandaged his wounds
READER 1: and treated them with oil and wine.
READER 2: He put him on his own donkey
JESUS: and took him to an inn where he could receive care.
READER 1: The next day the Samaritan said to the innkeeper,
READER 2: Look after him.
JESUS: This Samaritan paid the innkeeper two silver coins.
READER 1: He also promised to reimburse the innkeeper
READER 2: for any extra expense.

JESUS: Which of these men was a neighbor?
READER 1: The priest?
READER 2: The Levite?
JESUS: The Samaritan?
AUDIENCE: The one who had mercy on him.

JESUS: Go and do likewise,
READER 1: which the lawyer probably did not do
READER 2: but many of Jesus' followers have done since.

37

The Rich Fool

Scriptural Base: Luke 12
Subject: Focus of life, Perspective on wealth

Background of the Selection

Settling an inheritance dispute when a family member dies can be a great source of irritation, especially if that person was one of great means. The Rich Fool tells of a person who has plenty but wants more, presumably without altruistic reasons. The parable does not condemn wealth but rather focuses on wealth—where wealth becomes all-consuming. Jesus' story put wealth into its proper perspective.

Ideas for Reading

Participants: READER 1, READER 2, JESUS, and AUDIENCE.

The AUDIENCE plays the rich fool in this reading. The AUDIENCE should convey a feeling of arrogance as they read. The two READERS are separated by JESUS. JESUS should speak his lines slowly and deliberately.

The Rich Fool

READER 1: As Jesus taught his disciples one day
READER 2: about the kingdom—
READER 1: The crowd of many thousands pressed about him
READER 2: to the point of trampling one another.

READER 1: Jesus spoke of the yeast of the Pharisees—
JESUS: Beware of their hypocrisy.
READER 2: Jesus spoke of God's memory—

JESUS: Hairs and sparrows are numbered.
READER 1: Jesus spoke people who resist the Holy Spirit.

JESUS: They cannot be forgiven.
READER 2: He told his disciples
READER 1: not to fear the rulers or authorities.
JESUS: The Holy Spirit will teach you!

READER 2: In the midst of all this teaching,
READER 1: a man from the crowd,
READER 2: interested in fairness, said,
AUDIENCE: Teacher, tell my brother—
JESUS: Yes
AUDIENCE: Tell my brother to divide the inheritance with me.
JESUS: Man, who appointed me a judge between you?

READER 1: Then he said to him—
JESUS: Watch out!
AUDIENCE: Watch out for what?
JESUS: All kinds of greed.

AUDIENCE: But what of my inheritance?
READER 2: Since a man's life does not consist in the abundance of his possessions,
READER 1: Jesus told them a story—
READER 2: About riches, crops, barns, greed and eternal life.

JESUS: The farm of a certain rich man produced a good crop.
READER 1: So the rich man thought to himself,
AUDIENCE: What shall I do?
READER 2: Since he had no place to store all his crops, he said,
AUDIENCE: I will tear down my barns.

READER 2: And so he did and built bigger ones.
READER 1: He took all his grains and goods to the bigger barns
READER 2: and said to his servants,
AUDIENCE: Store them! Now I have plenty.

READER 1: His life from then on was very easy.
AUDIENCE: I eat, drink and have fun.
JESUS: You fool! This very night you will die.
AUDIENCE: Die?
JESUS: And who will get what you have stored for yourself?

READER 2: And so Jesus taught a profound lesson—
READER 1: Our greatest fear is not of ruler and authorities.
AUDIENCE: Then who or what?
JESUS: You yourself! Though life's choices you can destroy your soul.
READER 2: Which gives more and more meaning to the words of Jesus,
JESUS: If you have done it to the least of these people you have done it me.

38

Waiting and Being Ready

Scriptural Base: Luke 12
Subject: Second coming, Faithfulness, Being ready

Background of the Selection

This reading speaks to the question of being ready for the master's return. "What do I do in life while he tarries?" This question confronts every Christian who thinks about such things. We see examples here of individuals who waited and what they did while they waited.

Ideas for Reading

Participants: READER 1, READER 2, and AUDIENCE.

The AUDIENCE plays a person waiting joyfully for the return of the Lord. Their voices reflect an anticipation and joy as they read. READERS I and 2 carries the storyline and questions the AUDIENCE. The questions should be asked in a very pointed manner. Both READERS can stand close together but should not use the same microphone or look at the same section of the AUDIENCE.

Waiting and Being Ready

READER 1: Why are you waiting here?
AUDIENCE: I'm waiting for my master to return.
READER 2: You're just standing here!
AUDIENCE: My lamps are burning.
READER 1: When he comes and knocks then what?
AUDIENCE: I'll open the door for him!
READER 2: When do you expect him?
AUDIENCE: Anytime now.
READER 1: Anytime?
AUDIENCE: Yes.

READER 2: If he comes in at two o'clock in the morning
READER 1: will you be sleeping?
AUDIENCE: Yes, but my clothes are ready.
READER 2: I see the food is ready—
AUDIENCE: We will eat together.
READER 1: He will come! Are you ready to wait on him?
AUDIENCE: Yes.

READER 1: It will be good for you
READER 2: when the master finds you prepared when he comes.
READER 1: What if he comes at four o'clock in the morning?
AUDIENCE: I'll be ready.
READER 1: It's one thing if you are owner of the house
READER 2: and know what hour the thief was coming.
READER 1: You would not allow your house to be broken into.
AUDIENCE: I must be ready all the time!

READER 2: The master may come at an hour
READER 1: when you do not expect him.
READER 2: Who then is the faithful and eager?
AUDIENCE: The one who is always ready!
READER 1: It will be good for that person who watches.

READER 2: The Lord will put him in charge of all his possessions.
READER 1: But what of the person who thinks his master delays?

AUDIENCE: **They take advantage of the employees.**
READER 1: They overwork the men,
READER 2: and harass the women.
READER 1: They eat and drink and get drunk—
READER 2: They will be cut to pieces and assigned a place with the unbelievers.
READER 1: Blessed is the person, who listens to the Master,
READER 2: daily watching and waiting.

READER 1: Joseph of Arimathea,
READER 2: a prominent member of the Council—
READER 1: Waiting for the kingdom of God—
READER 2: Was ready to take the body of Jesus.

READER 1: Zechariah, a priest—
READER 2: Waiting and hoping in the temple—
READER 1: Was ready for the Messiah!

READER 2: Simeon, a good man—
READER 1: waiting for the consolation of Israel—
READER 2: through his devotion
READER 1: was ready for the Messiah.

READER 2: Abraham, the father of nations—
READER 1: Waiting patiently for a son—
READER 2: Was ready and he received the promise.
READER 1: And now what are you waiting for?
AUDIENCE: **I confess my sins.**

READER 2: Be baptized.
READER 1: Have your sins washed away.
AUDIENCE: **Save me, Oh Lord.**

READER 2: You are now ready for Jesus to come.
READER 1: Christ sacrificed once to take away sin,
READER 2: and he will appear a second time,
READER 1: not to bear sin,
READER 2: but to bring salvation
READER 1: to those who are ready and waiting for him.

39

The Rich Man and Lazarus

Scriptural Base: Luke 16
Subject: Relation to the poor, Decision making

Background of the Selection

The parable of the Rich Man and Lazarus speaks with such detail that many find it had to believe it is just a story. A popular story of the time, Jesus' parable shows that we are responsible for the decisions we make here and now. There will be no second chance. The Israelites knew what it meant to be poor and to be rich. This reading assumes that the story is a metaphor and suggests that attitudes toward our fellow human do not change in heaven or hell.

Ideas for Reading

Participants: READER 1, READER 2, LAZARUS, and AUDIENCE.

The AUDIENCE plays the rich man in the parable. The voice should connote arrogance and snobbery throughout the entire reading. LAZARUS should be positioned in front of the AUDIENCE away from the two READERS. In this reading the READERS need to be close together. If microphones are used the READERS should use separate ones.

The Rich Man and Lazarus

READER 1: There was a man
READER 2: who was very rich.
AUDIENCE: l am that man.
READER 1: He wore fine clothes
READER 2: and lived in luxury everyday.
AUDIENCE: I do lead a good life.

READER 1: There was another man
READER 2: who was very poor.
LAZARUS: My name is Lazarus.
AUDIENCE: He is just a beggar!
READER 2: He wore rags for clothes
READER 1: and had no place to stay.
AUDIENCE: Let him live at my gate.
LAZARUS: I am so grateful.

READER 1: Lazarus was also a sick man.
LAZARUS: I am covered with sores.
AUDIENCE: Disgusting—let the dogs lick his sores.
READER 2: He was also in need of food.
LAZARUS: I am hungry.
AUDIENCE: Eat my crumbs!
LAZARUS: You are very kind.

READER 1: No matter how rich
READER 2: or how poor people are
READER 1: they all must eventually die.

READER 2: After death Lazarus went to Abraham's side.
LAZARUS: Peace at last.
READER 1: The rich man went to hell
READER 2: where he was tormented day and night.
AUDIENCE: I want to go back to earth.

READER 1: In his torment the rich man looked up
READER 2: and saw by the side of Abraham—
AUDIENCE: Lazarus?!

READER 1: So the rich man called to Abraham.
AUDIENCE: Send Lazarus with water.
READER 2: Abraham answered,
READER 1: Son, do you remember your lifetime?
AUDIENCE: Have Lazarus bring water.
READER 2: In your life you lived in luxury.
READER 1: You gave dog's tongues for sores,
READER 2: the gate for a roof,
READER 1: and crumbs for food.
AUDIENCE: I am in agony in this fire.

READER 1: You made a gulf between you and Lazarus.
READER 2: A gulf made by wanting and getting,
READER 1: ignoring and forgetting,
READER 2: seeing and neglecting.
READER 1: Even in hell you still want!
AUDIENCE: I beg you to send Lazarus.
READER 1: The gulf you created on earth is still present in hell.
READER 2: You want Lazarus to come to you.
READER 1: You want Lazarus to bring water to you.
READER 2: You want water for your tongue.

AUDIENCE: Then send Lazarus to my brothers.
READER 1: And now you want Lazarus to go to your brothers. Why?
READER 2: You and your brothers
READER 1: have not seen the homeless.
AUDIENCE 1: But we have eyes!

READER 2: You and your brothers
READER 1: have not heard the pain of those who have sores.
AUDIENCE: But we have ears!

READER 2: You and your brothers
READER 1: have not followed the hungry.
AUDIENCE: **But we have legs!**

READER 2: Neither you nor your brothers
READER 1: have heard, seen, nor followed
READER 2: the God of Moses
READER 1: or the God of the Prophets.
READER 2: Even now you would rather stay in hell
READER 1: and have Lazarus serve you
READER 2: than to be with Lazarus at Abraham's side.
READER 1: On earth you did not see death in the life of Lazarus
READER 2: then nor now do you see life in the death of God.
AUDIENCE: Send Lazarus with water!

40

The Lepers

Scriptural Base: Luke 17
Subject: Forgiveness, Trust, Thankfulness

Background of the Selection

In the narrative of the lepers we see a simple story of forgiveness. The ten lepers were joined together as a result of their leprosy and once healed had no regard for one another or for the healer. The case of the Samaritan was different! He returned to thank the healer. In the excitement of being healed of the cursed leprosy only the Samaritan took the time and effort to give thanks. This approach to gifts and healings and answered prayer is often our approach today.

Ideas for Reading

Participants: READER 1, READER 2, SAMARITAN and AUDIENCE.

The AUDIENCE plays the lepers. The voices should indicate pity as they beg for healing. The voice changes to exuberance as they are healed and finally to arrogance as they find themselves as regular Jews. The two READERS will be separated by the SAMARITAN. The SAMARITAN reads along with the AUDIENCE. His "Thank you" is the only fine spoken by him alone. He should speak with his head lifted upward to heaven. He stands between the two READERS. Each has a microphone.

The Lepers

READER 1: On his way to Jerusalem
READER 2: Jesus traveled along the border
READER 1: between Samaria and Galilee.

READER 2: There stood ten men—
AUDIENCE: Jesus—
READER 1: They called in a loud voice.
AUDIENCE: Master—
READER 2: Trying to get the attention of Jesus—
AUDIENCE: Have pity on us.
READER 1: They were indeed pitiful.
READER 2: Go show yourself to the priest.

READER 1: They went.
READER 2: They were healed.
AUDIENCE: We are cleansed!

READER 1: One of them—
AUDIENCE: We are free!
READER 2: saw he was healed—
AUDIENCE: We are all heated!
READER 1: came back
READER 2: threw himself at Jesus' feet
READER 1: and thanked him
READER 2: in a very loud voice.

READER 1: Just one came back
READERS 1, 2: and he was a Samaritan!
SAMARITAN: Thank you, Lord.
READER 1: The other nine were—
AUDIENCE: We are Jews!
READER 1: but only the foreigner—
SAMARITAN: Thank you Lord—
READER 2: Returned to praise God.
AUDIENCE: We are Jews!

READER 1: And to untold generations
READER 2: this story tells
READER 1: of faithfulness
READER 2: and thankfulness
READER 1: of God's true followers.

41

Nathan and David

Scriptural Base: I Samuel 12
Subject: Kindness, Consistency, Greed

Background of the Selection

David had tasted the wealth of the land through the blessing of the Lord. As with wealth often comes power and that was certainly true in David's case. He thought he could have another man's wife with no penalty or punishment because he was king. David took Bathsheba for his wife and in the process killed her legitimate husband. The Lord rebuked him through this simple story delivered by Nathan.

Ideas for Reading

Participants: READER 1, READER 2, AUDIENCE 1, AUDIENCE 1, and DAVID.

AUDIENCE 1 plays the rich man. AUDIENCE 1 should act sure of themselves which will translate as arrogance throughout the reading. AUDIENCE 2 plays the poor man. AUDIENCE 2 reads with hopelessness in the voice. DAVID'S lines are to be read with rage. After DAVID'S outburst of an answer there is a pause, then the READERS softly but firmly read the last three lines.

Nathan and David

READER 1: Nathan, a prophet of God,
READER 2: told David the king this very simple story
READER 1: for a very good reason.

READER 2: In a certain town
READER 1: there were two men.
AUDIENCE 1: I am very rich.
AUDIENCE 2: I am very poor.
AUDIENCE 1: I have very large herds.
READER 1: He had herds of cattle and sheep
READER 2: which made him very, very rich!

READER 1: The poor man had
AUDIENCE 2: I have nothing!
READER 1: He had nothing but, one, only one ewe
READER 2: which still made him very poor.
READER 1: This one little ewe
AUDIENCE 2: is like a daughter to me.
READER 1: Indeed it was, for the ewe ate at his table
READER 2: drank from his cup
READER 1: and slept in his arms.

READER 2: The rich man was not only rich but very powerful.
READER 1: He took the man's little ewe—
AUDIENCE 1: Slaughter it. Dress it.
AUDIENCE 2: It is all that I have.
AUDIENCE 1: Let's eat!
READER 2: He partied with his friends.

READER 1: Although the rich man had plenty—
READER 2: Plenty of ewes.
READER 1: Plenty of lambs.
READER 2: Plenty of sheep.
READER 1: Plenty of goats.
READER 2: Plenty of everything.
AUDIENCE 1: I still want more.

READER 2: He wanted the best
READER 1: of what others had!
READER 2: He had wealth.
AUDIENCE 2: But I have no wealth.
AUDIENCE 1: I also have power.
READER 2: With his power and wealth
READER 1: he took advantage of the very poor man's poverty.

DAVID: The story makes me angry! Who is this man?
READER 1: It made him really mad!
READER 2: David began to rant and rave—
READER 1: And so he should have.
DAVID: If there is a God and surely there is—
READER 2: said David,
DAVID: this rich man deserves to die! He must pay for the lamb
four times over. Who is this man?
READER 1: David.
READER 2: David.
READERS 1, 2: You, are that man!

42

Why O Lord?

Scriptural Base: Psalm 2
Subject: Trust in the Lord, Angry God, Safety in God

Background of the Selection

This psalm shows the futility of universal rebellion against the Lord. It shows that those who put their faith in God will find happiness. The psalm shows how humankind has developed a disdain for God. It also shows God's attitude toward their taunts as he establishes his kingship and reclaims ownership of this earth. There is the hope that all is well for those who put their trust in God.

Ideas for Reading

Participants: READER 1, READER 2, and AUDIENCE.

The AUDIENCE plays a commentator on the descriptions of the nations and evil people. They are God's representative on earth. The READERS give the background material and their part should be read with intensity. Much of the AUDIENCE parts should be read in doubt and concern.

Why O Lord?

READER 1: Why, O Lord?
AUDIENCE: Yes, why—
READER 2: Do the nations rage?
READER 1: Why do the nations conspire when the Lord in heaven just laughs?
AUDIENCE: Why—
READER 2: Do the people plot in vain
READER 1: when the Lord just scoffs?
AUDIENCE: Why—
READER 2: Do kings and rulers gather together against the Lord?
AUDIENCE: He should rebuke them in anger!

READER 1: He terrifies them in his wrath.
READER 2: They try to break their chains
READER 1: and throw off their fetters.
AUDIENCE: Then the Lord still reigns!

READER 2: Here is what the Lord says to you:
READER 1: You are my Son.
READER 2: I have become your Father.
READER 1: Ask of me and you will find your inheritance.
READER 2: Ask of me and you will find a place to rule.
AUDIENCE: He has made me a king?

READER 1: Be wise you rulers of the earth.
READER 2: Rejoice with trembling.
READER 1: His wrath can flare at any time
READER 2: and in a moment you will be destroyed in your way.

READER 1: Blessed are all who take refuge in him.
AUDIENCE: I will serve the Lord with fear.

43

Who May Live?

Scriptural Base: Psalm 15
Subject: God's Blessings, Christian Virtues

Background of the Selection

Psalm 15 is a well-known psalm. It is said that the 613 commandments of the Pentateuch are contained in this one Psalm. The Psalmist asks a series of questions that he immediately answers. The answers profile what God requires of his people.

Ideas for Reading

Participants: READER 1, READER 2, AUDIENCE 1, AUDIENCE 2.

AUDIENCE 1 and AUDIENCE 2 ask God some questions with an occasional statement. READERS 1 and 2 play the role of God. Their part needs to be read intensely and confidently. Although it is effective to have the readers seen on the platform, having the READERS not seen can add a new dynamic to the interactive reading. If the voices of the READERS are from offstage then the audience ought to be informed of it before the reading begins.

Who May Live?

AUDIENCE 1: Lord, O Lord,
AUDIENCE 2: who may live in your sanctuary?
AUDIENCE 1: God, O God,
AUDIENCE 2: who may exist in your lovely dwelling?
READER 2: Those who walk blamelessly
READER 1: and do what is righteous.

AUDIENCE 2: Who may live with you?
READER 2: The ones who speak the truth from the heart
READER 1: and never, never slander with the tongue.
AUDIENCE 1: Who may live with God?
READER 1: The person who does the neighbor no wrong,
READER 2: including casting no slurs or passing on gossip.
READER 1: The people who live forever in God's presence despise vile people,
READER 2: but they honor those who fear the Lord.

AUDIENCE 2: Who may have eternal life?
READER 1: The ones who are truthful even when it hurts.
READER 2: People who lend money without high interest.
READER 1: Anyone who does not accept a bribe against the innocent.
READER 2: When you do these things
READER 1: you will never be shaken, because you dwell in my presence.
READER 2: You will live with me in my sanctuary, in my presence forever.
READER 1: You will have eternal life. You will never die.

AUDIENCE 1: That which we want to do,
AUDIENCE 2: we don't do!
AUDIENCE 1: That which we don't want to do,
AUDIENCE 2: we do!

AUDIENCE 1: How then do we walk blamelessly?
AUDIENCE 2: How do we not lie and slander?
AUDIENCE 1: Gossip and bribe?
AUDIENCE 2: Tell us how to be righteous
AUDIENCE 1: and despise the vile?

READER 1: I will keep you strong to the end,
READER 2: so you will be blameless on the day of my coming.
READER 1: I have chosen you to be holy and blameless.
READER 2: Now so live!

44

The Heavens Declare

Scriptural Base: Psalm 19
Subject: Praise, Nature, God's law

Background of the Selection

Psalm 19 is another well-known nature psalms. In this psalm nature and revelation testify of God's love. This meditative psalm combines God's self-revelation, the world of nature and His law. The Psalmist features the spectacle of the starry sky that makes humankind seem very small. He asserts that the moral law gives humanity its dignity and intelligence.

Ideas for Reading

Participants: READER 1, READER 2, and AUDIENCE.

The AUDIENCE and the two READERS interact in a litany of praise and appreciation of the wonders of the universe and God's law.

The Heavens Declare

READER 1: The heavens—
READER 2: above and around us—
READER 1: speak to us.
AUDIENCE: They declare the God of glory.
READER 1: The skies—
READER 2: what do they proclaim?
AUDIENCE: His hands at work.

READER 1: Day after day and night after night
READER 2: these heavens and skies give us
AUDIENCE: knowledge and wisdom.
READER 1: There is no speech
READER 2: or language
READER 1: where their voice is not heard.
READER 2: The voice of knowledge
READER 1: goes out into all the earth
READER 2: and the words to the ends of the world—
READER 1: Just as the heavens declare the voice of knowledge—
READER 2: and it goes out to all the universe
READER 1: so do His laws teach
READER 2: and instruct everywhere.

READER 1: The law of the Lord—what does it declare?
AUDIENCE: Perfection and renewal.
READER 2: The statutes of the Lord—what do they proclaim?
AUDIENCE: Trust worthiness and wisdom.
READER 1: The precepts of the Lord—what do they give?
AUDIENCE: Joy to the heart.
READER 2: The commands of the Lord?
AUDIENCE: Give light to the eyes.

READER 1: The fear of the Lord is pure, enduring forever.
READER 2: The ordinances of the Lord are altogether sure and righteous,
READER 1: His commands are more precious than gold.
AUDIENCE: More than much fine gold!

READER 2: His statutes are sweeter than honey.
AUDIENCE: Sweeter than the honeycomb!
READER 1: What is within the law and the precepts?
AUDIENCE: Warnings and a great reward!
READER 2: The Lord's instructions
AUDIENCE: Discern errors…and…reveal hidden faults.

READER 1: His commands will keep you from
AUDIENCE: Willful sins!
READER 2: His precepts prevent sins from ruling the life—
AUDIENCE: I can be blameless?
READER 1: and innocent of great transgression.
READER 2: You are free, free at last.

READER 1: Then may the words and the meditations
READER 2: of my heart and thoughts
AUDIENCE: be pleasing in your sight,
READER 1: O Lord.
READER 2: My Rock.
AUDIENCE: My Redeemer.

45

The Lord Answers

Scriptural Base: Psalm 20
Subject: Courage, Cry for Help, Trust in God

Background of the Selection

This psalm was composed to be sung on behalf of the king who was about to go war. Some think that the psalm was written about the time that David was going to war with the Syrians and Ammonites. The author acknowledges that victory is the Lord's in spite of the armament.

Ideas for Reading

Participants: READER 1, READER 2, and AUDIENCE.

All three entities are involved in a communal prayer and statement of faith and confidences in the leading of God. This reading is to be read as if one person were speaking.

The Lord Answers

READER 1: The Lord, the Creator God—
AUDIENCE: answers and protects
READER 2: while he sends and grants,
READER 1: remembers and accepts.
READER 2: And finally he gives and makes.

READER 1: May the Lord answer you—
AUDIENCE: We are in stress.
READER 1: in your time of need.
AUDIENCE: We have sorrow and sadness.
READER 1: May the name of the God of Jacob protect you.
AUDIENCE: Protect us from our sins and cynicisms and ourselves.
READER 2: May he send you help in trials and troubles.
AUDIENCE: Grant us support.

READER 1: May he remember all your sacrifices.
AUDIENCE: Accept our offerings.
READER 2: May he give you the desire of your heart.
AUDIENCE: Make our plans succeed.
READER 1: You, the work of His hand, will
AUDIENCE: shout and lift.
READER 2: Then you will
AUDIENCE: call and request.

READER 1: And at times you will—
AUDIENCE: Fall!
READER 2: But you will rise because,
AUDIENCE: I know and trust.

READER 1: You will shout for joy when you are victorious
READER 2: and you will lift up your banners in the name of our God.
AUDIENCE: Lord, grant all our requests.

READER 1: Now you know that the Lord saves his anointed.
READER 2: He answers him from his holy heaven with the saving power of his right hand.

READER 1: Some trust in chariots,

READER 2: some in horses and armies.

AUDIENCE: We trust in the name of the Lord.

READER 2: Some are brought to their knees and fall.

AUDIENCE: We rise up and stand firm.

READER 1: O Lord, answer

AUDIENCE: Answer us when we call!

46

The Lord is My Shepherd

Scriptural Base: Psalm 23
Subject: Gods care, Faithfulness of God, Triumph of the righteous

Background of the Selection

The twenty-third Psalm is so well-known that many could repeat it without even thinking about the words let alone the meaning. While the setting of the writing was from an agricultural economy, it still has meaning to us today. Indeed its meaning transcends time and culture. The psalm tells of a caring God as a gracious host and constant companion. In an effort to cause readers to rethink their relationship to God, the chapter can be restructured to cause the respondents to interact with God.

Ideas for Reading

Participants: READER, and AUDIENCE.

In this reading the AUDIENCE plays one of the sheep, a person facing death, and a beneficiary of God gifts. The AUDIENCE answers to God, the true Shepherd. The AUDIENCE will actually complete some sentences of God. This will show that the recipients of God's care know him and can even predict his responses. The one READER plays God. The READER uses a voice that is tender yet authoritative.

The Lord is My Shepherd

READER: I am the Lord, you shall not want.
AUDIENCE: You are my Shepherd.
READER: I will restore your soul
AUDIENCE: by lying down in green pastures.

READER: I will renew your spirits
AUDIENCE: by leading me beside quiet waters.
READER: You may pass through the valley of death.
AUDIENCE: With you, I will fear no evil,
READER: I will comfort you with my rod and staff.
AUDIENCE: Be with me!

READER: I will guide you in paths of righteousness for my name's sake. A table is prepared for you.
AUDIENCE: I will without fear eat in the presence of my enemies?
READER: Your head is anointed with oil.
AUDIENCE: My cup overflows!
READER: All the days of your life you will be followed by
AUDIENCE: goodness and love
READER: and with me
AUDIENCE: I will dwell forever.

47

The Lord is My Salvation

Scriptural Base: Palm 27
Subject: Salvation, Trust in the Lord, Help in time of need

Background of the Selection

David wrote this psalm when he was a hunted runaway, finding asylum in the rocks and caves of the wilderness. It reveals the psalmist's spirit of complete confidence in God in spite of difficulty. The psalmist expresses confidence in God, the cry for help and finally the hopeful trust in God as the solution.

Ideas for Reading

Participants: READER 1, READER 2, and AUDIENCE.

The AUDIENCE plays the writer of the psalm. The two READERS give the background for the troubles and solutions.

The Lord is My Salvation

READER 1: The Lord is light and salvation.
AUDIENCE: Then whom shall I fear?

READER 2: The Lord is the stronghold of life.
AUDIENCE: So of whom shall I be afraid?

READER 1: Evil men will advance to devour
READER 2: and enemies and foes will attack,
AUDIENCE: They will stumble and fall.

READER 1: Armies will besiege.
AUDIENCE: But I am confident.
READER 2: Wars will break out.
AUDIENCE: But my heart will not fear.

READER 1: Ask of the Lord,
AUDIENCE: May I dwell in your house?
READER 2: Seek the Lord and you will find.
AUDIENCE: May I gaze upon Your beauty?

READER 1: There are days of trouble.
AUDIENCE: Keep me safe, Lord.
READER 2: There are hours of tribulation,
AUDIENCE: but God hides me.

READER 2: There are moments of temptation.
AUDIENCE: Set me on a high rock.
READER 1: Enemies will surround!
AUDIENCE: Exalt me above them!

READER 1: His tabernacle is filled with singing and music.
AUDIENCE: Take my sacrifice with shouts of joy.
READER 2: The Lord is merciful and answers.
AUDIENCE: Hear my voice.

READER 1: The Lord is a helper and a Savior.
AUDIENCE: He will not reject me.
READER 2: Fathers and mothers, will forsake.
AUDIENCE: Lord, you always receive me.

READER 1: The Lord leads in straight paths because of oppressors.
AUDIENCE: Teach me your way.
READER 2: False witnesses arise
READER 1: breathing out violence and desiring harm.
AUDIENCE: Lord don't allow them their desires.
READER 2: In the land of the living, the goodness of the Lord can be seen.
AUDIENCE: And I am confident of this.
READER 1: Be patient, be strong and take heart.
AUDIENCE: I will wait for the Lord, for he is my salvation.

48

The Great Hope

Scriptural Base: Scripture
Subject: Second Coming, Promises of God, A redeeming God

Background of the Selection

Scripture continually promises the second coming of Jesus. The fulfillment of this promise can be realized only through the grace and power of God. Words such as grace, glory and power create a desire in the Christian's heart to be a part of the plan of God forever. This reading brings these words and ideas together.

Ideas for Reading

Participants: READER 1, READER 2, and AUDIENCE.

The AUDIENCE takes part in reading that stresses the attribute of God with the final desire for him to come to this earth. It should be read with voices filled with adoration and praise.

The Great Hope

READER 1: Grace to you.
AUDIENCE: Peace to you.
READER 1, 2: Grace and peace to you,
READER 1: from him who was,
READER 2: from him who is to come,
AUDIENCE: from him who is.

READER 1: Grace to you
AUDIENCE: from our Lord.
READER 1: Grace and peace to you
AUDIENCE: from our Lord and Savior.
READER 1: Grace and peace to you
AUDIENCE: from our Lord and Savior Jesus Christ!

READER 1: Glory be given
READER 2: to him who loves you,
AUDIENCE: who has freed you,
READER 2: who keeps you,
READER 1: by his power.

AUDIENCE: He keeps you from falling.
READER 1: He made you to be a kingdom of priests
AUDIENCE: to serve God the Father.
READER 1: To him who presents you without fault and with joy
AUDIENCE: to the only God our Savior.
READER 2: To him be glory,
AUDIENCE: and majesty,
READER 2: and authority,
AUDIENCE: and power,
READER 2: now
AUDIENCE: and forever and ever!

READER 1: Look,
AUDIENCE: Every eye shall see him.
READER 2: Listen.
AUDIENCE: The trumpet shall sound.

READER 1: He is coming with the clouds,
AUDIENCE: We shall meet him in the air.

READER 1: Glory and honor to Him
READER 2: who presents you without fault,
AUDIENCE: without blemish
READER 2: and with great joy.
AUDIENCE: Even so, come Lord Jesus.

49

Mizpah

Scriptural Base: Genesis 31
Subject: Reconciliation

Background of the Selection

Jacob and Laban had left one another with ill feeling between them. The hatred was so great that Jacob took steps to protect part of his family by dividing them into separate camps and positioning them at different locations. The meeting between the son-in-law and the father-in-law was tense at first but not acrimonious. It ended in the joint statement of a pledge of peace between the two.

Ideas for Reading

Participants: READER, AUDIENCE.

The AUDIENCE plays Laban and the READER plays Jacob. The voices need to reflect a reconciliation of two foes in this dialogue.

Mizpah

READER: May the Lord bless you
AUDIENCE: and bless both of us
READER: and keep both of us while we are absent one from another. May the Lord make his face shine
AUDIENCE: shine on all of us
READER: while we are absent one from another. May the Lord lift up his countenance upon you
AUDIENCE: and give us peace
READER: while we are absent one from another.

READER: Grace be to you
AUDIENCE: and to you and to all of us.
READER: May the Lord provide you with good health.
AUDIENCE: May you walk in the truth
READER: as Jesus is in the truth, while we are absent one from another.

READER: May the Lord watch
AUDIENCE: watch between you and me
READER: while we are absent one from another. May we be faithful,
AUDIENCE: faithful in his mercy.

READER: May the Lord grant you love,
AUDIENCE: love to one another,
READER: even unto the uttermost parts of the earth
AUDIENCE: while we are absent one from another.

50

Abraham

Scriptural Base: Genesis 22
Subject: Trust, Faith, Obedience, The True God

Background of the Selection

In an effort to teach Abraham his true character, God asked Abraham to sacrifice his only son Isaac. Abraham did not find it easy to carry out the command of God because this son was the child of his and Sarah's old age. God set up a plan to teach Abraham that Yahweh was the God of life, not death.

Ideas for Reading

Participants: READER 1, READER 2, and ABRAHAM.

The audience reads the part of ABRAHAM. The voice of ABRAHAM needs to express the emotions of ABRAHAM, which should range from thankfulness to dismay to thankfulness. Mention to the audience the pause in the reading and that the two short sentences need to be read quietly with dismay and questioning. Before READER 2 delivers the last line there needs to be a pause.

Or—The AUDIENCE can be split into two parts with half one (READER 1) read by AUDIENCE 1 and half two (READER 2) read by AUDIENCE 2. In this case there would be no one on the platform except the person reading the ABRAHAM lines. As the ABRAHAM lines are read the reader would turn the head slightly to give the impression that God is mysteriously speaking to him.

Abraham

READER 1: Abraham,
ABRAHAM: Yes, Lord.
READER 2: Abraham do you love. me.
ABRAHAM: Why yes, Lord.
READER 1: Abraham, do you trust me.
ABRAHAM: Lord, yes!
READER 2: Abraham, are you pleased with your son.
ABRAHAM: I am pleased, Lord.

READER 1: Abraham, take your son and go.
ABRAHAM: I'll go, Lord.
READER 2: Go to the region of Moriah.
ABRAHAM: Yes—
READER 1: Sacrifice Isaac, your son, there.
ABRAHAM: But—
READER 2: Sacrifice him there on one of the mountains.

ABRAHAM: Sacrifice my only son?
READER 1: Sacrifice your only son Isaac—
ABRAHAM: Sacrifice the son of the promise?
READER 2: Yes, sacrifice your only son.
ABRAHAM: *(pause then say quietly)* Sacrifice my son! Sacrifice my only son?

READER 1: So Abraham went
READER 2: the very next morning
READER 1: with donkey,
READER 2: servants,
READER 1: wood,
READER 2: fire,
READER 1: knife,
READER 2: and Isaac,
READER 1: but with no lamb.

READER 2: After several days
READER 1: of traveling,
READER 2: of thinking,

READER 1: of hoping,
READER 2: of wishing
READER 1: Abraham took the knife
READER 2: to slay his son.

READER 1: Abraham! Abraham!
ABRAHAM: Yes, Lord.
READERS 1, 2: Do not lay a hand on the boy.
READER 2: I have provided the lamb.

51

Celebrate God

Scriptural Base: Psalms 147–150
Subject: Happiness of the believer, Celebrating God's goodness

Background of the Selection

Expressions of gloom and dismay fill the Psalms but so do expressions of celebration and honor to God. Psalms 147–150 show some good examples of these positive characteristics as such provide a fitting conclusion to the book of Psalms. Celebrating God's goodness includes the entire creative expression of humanity. This reading should celebrate.

Ideas for Reading

Participants: READER 1, READER 2, and AUDIENCE.

The AUDIENCE and READERS combine their voices in praising God. Encourage the AUDIENCE to read with a festive voice.

Celebrate God

READER 1: It is so good to celebrate God's presence!
READER 2: It is so good to sing his praises all day!
AUDIENCE: Let's celebrate what he has done!

READER 1: He has done so much for you—
AUDIENCE: Created the world.
READER 1: Made the sun and moon.
READER 2: Lighted unnumbered stars in the universe.
READER 1: Put creatures that swim and crawl
READER 2: and walk and fly upon our earth.
AUDIENCE: We all enjoy these gifts!

READER 1: Praise him also for his devoted servants:
READER 2: who have communicated his word,
READER 1: who have performed his miracles,
READER 2: who have brought his healing to people's hurts.
AUDIENCE: They bless our lives!

READER 1: God still blesses your world—
READER 2: Flowers bloom in glorious color.
READER 1: Rains freshen the earth.
READER 2: Birds fill the air with song.
AUDIENCE: Thanks be to God for his perpetual love!

READER 2: He loves you!
READER 1: He pursues those of you who run from him.
READER 2: He reaches out to heal you and to draw you to himself.
AUDIENCE: He has forgiven us! Praise God!

READER 1: He is worthy of your praise.
AUDIENCE: We will proclaim his love!
READER 2: Singing his glories to all.
READER 1: Those of you who write or paint,
READER 2: write and paint of the Lord.

READER 1: Those of you who dance and play,
READER 2: dance and play of the Lord.
AUDIENCE: Let's celebrate!

READER 1: Celebrate with music, poetry and art!
READER 2: Let's all join in celebrating the majesty of our great and loving God.
AUDIENCE: Let's celebrate God!

52

From Gloom to Glory

Scriptural Base: The Psalm
Subject: Salvation, Forgiveness, Redemption, Grace

Background of the Selection

Scripture is filled with descriptions of the human condition: sins, injustice, evil, oppression, revolt, and cruelty. But the purpose for this recitation centers in the message of a way out. This reading chronicles a long list of human depravity only to open up the redemptive plan of God. Thank God that over all the gloom hang his promises.

Ideas for Reading

Participants: READER 1, READER 2, READER 3, and AUDIENCE.

The AUDIENCE asks the questions: How do you get out of the gloom to glory? The READERS initially recount the iniquities of human beings but then explain the beauty of redemption and glory.

From Gloom to Glory

READER 1: Your sins
READER 2: have separated you from God.
READER 3: Your iniquities have hidden you
READER 2: from his face.
READER 3: You have gone astray!
AUDIENCE: Where is justice? It can't be far!
READER 1: Your tongue mutters wicked things.
READER 2: Few call for justice.
AUDIENCE: Where is righteousness? Is it not out of reach?

READER 1: Integrity—
READER 2: You do not plead with it,
READER 3: No one pleads for it.
READER 2: Your arguments are empty.
READER 1: You speak lies.
READER 3: You conceive evil.
AUDIENCE: We are looking for the light!

READER 2: All is darkness.
READER 3: You walk in deep shadows like the blind.
READER 1: You grope along a wall.
READER 2: You travel by feeling.
READER 3: You are people without eyes.
READER 1: You walk at midday as if it were twilight.
READER 2: Among the strong you are like the dead.
AUDIENCE: We are looking for justice and righteousness and life.

READER 2: You growl like bears.
READER 1: You mourn like doves.
AUDIENCE: Please show us justice?
READER 2: You can't find it.
READER 3: You—
READER 2: You dress in cobwebs
READER 1: and it does not cover.
READER 2: Your deeds are evil.
READER 3: Your acts are violent.

READER 2: Your feet rush to sin.
READER 1: Your hands shed innocent blood.
READER 2: You thoughts are evil.
AUDIENCE: We are looking for peace!

READER 3: There is no peace.
READER 1: Your roads are crooked.
READER 2: The path leads to destruction.
AUDIENCE: Where is deliverance?
READER 3: It is too far away.
AUDIENCE: Where can we find forgiveness?
READER 2: Your offenses are too many,
READER 1: they are ever with us.
READER 2: Your sins—
AUDIENCE: Can we look to the Lord?

READER 3: Rebellion and treachery against the Lord
READER 1: is your way of life.
READER 2: Oppression,
READER 3: revolt,
READER 2: lies.
ALL READERS: This is your heart.
AUDIENCE: Righteousness—where are you?

READER 1: Righteousness!
READER 2: Righteousness stands a distance.
READER 3: Truth stumbles in the streets.
READER 2: Honesty cannot enter.
READER 1: Truth is nowhere.
READER 2: Whoever shuns evil becomes a prey.
AUDIENCE: Where is the Redeemer?

READER 2: Redeemer?
READER 1: There is no justice,
READER 2: there is no righteousness.
READER 3: Will you still come
READER 2: to repay for what has been done?
READER 1: Will you bring anger to the enemies?

READER 2: Retribution to foes?
AUDIENCE: **Look, the Redeemer has come to Zion!**

READER 1: The Redeemer has come to Zion!
READER 3: Do you repent?
AUDIENCE: **Forgive me. Fill me with glory.**

READER 1: Then arise, shine, for your light has come.
READER 2: Your walk is upright.
READER 3: Your hand helps.
READER 2: Now your feet rush to do good.
READER 1: Arise, shine, for your light has come,
READER 2: and the glory of the Lord rises upon you.
AUDIENCE: **The darkness of cruelty is gone!**

READER 2: The darkness of violence has left!
READER 3: The thick darkness of evil has departed!
AUDIENCE: **Glory shines all about!**
ALL READERS: Glory does shines all about!
AUDIENCE: **We will arise and shine**
ALL READERS: your light has come.
READER 1: Lift up your eyes and look about.
AUDIENCE: **We see the brightness of the dawn.**

READER 2: The fight is now yours.
AUDIENCE: **We are the dawn!**
READER 2: You are the brightness.
AUDIENCE: **Our eyes are opened.**
READER 2: Look at the promised land.
AUDIENCE: **We have been glorified.**
ALL READERS: We are glorified!
AUDIENCE: **We are free!**

READER 1: We have freedom!
AUDIENCE: **Our hearts throb with joy!**
READER 3: Your sons and daughters are with you. You look radiant!
AUDIENCE: **Our fight has come!!**
READER 1: The Redeemer has come to Zion.

AUDIENCE: The Redeemer has come to us.

READER 2: Give of your gold.

READER 3: Give of your frankincense.

READER 1: Give of your myrrh.

READER 2: Rejoice.

AUDIENCE: Salvation is ours!

ALL READERS: Let us all arise and shine.

READER 3: The light has come.

READER 1: We are free.

AUDIENCE: We are free at last.

53

Gratefulness

Scriptural Base: Scripture
Subject: Gratefulness

Background of the Selection

This reading is a combination of the Old and New Testament treatment on human gratefulness to God for his mercies and care. The Bible writers throughout present a consistent thread relating human obligation and its response to God.

Ideas for Reading

Participants: READER 1, READER 2, READER 3, AUDIENCE.

The AUDIENCE clings to the phrase "His loves endures forever" in this reading. READERS 1, 2, 3 ask questions and state facts. These parts should be read with feelings of love and thankfulness to God.

Gratefulness

READER 1: Give thanks to the Lord,
READER 2: call on his name,
READER 1: make known among the nations
READER 2: what he has done.
READER 1: Give thanks to the Lord.

READER 3: What of His love?
AUDIENCE: His love endures forever.
READER 3: With what shall we praise him?
READER 2: With trumpets and songs, with cymbals and harps,
READER 1: with voices and choirs, with other instruments,
READER 2: with sacrifices.
READER 3: What of his love?
AUDIENCE: His love endures forever.

READER 3: Why shall we thank him?
READER 1: Because he is our strength and shield.
READER 2: Because our hearts leap for joy
READER 1: we cannot be silent.
READER 2: We must tell of his wonderful deeds.
READER 3: Then tell of His love!
AUDIENCE: It endures forever.

READER 3: When shall we praise him?
READER 2: As you enter his gates proclaim thanksgiving.
READER 1: As you enter his courts shout praise.
READER 2: Let the sound of singing
READER 1: ever be on your lips.
READER 2: Give him thanks constantly.
READER 3: Tell the world
AUDIENCE: that his love endures forever.

READER 1: Thank him for his righteous laws.
READER 2: Thank him for becoming our salvation.
READER 1: His voice speaks to the penitent,
READER 2: then join in triumphal procession,

READER 1: eat His loaves and fishes,
READER 2: dine at the His last supper.
READER 3: Thank him and shout
AUDIENCE: His love endures forever.

READER 1: Jesus took the five loaves and two fishes
READER 2: Thank you for the food we eat.
READER 1: Jesus took the bread and the wine
READER 3: Accept our gratitude.
READER 2: Jesus fed them at Tiberias.
READER 1: Thanks be to God.
READER 3: He feeds us today because
AUDIENCE: His love endures forever!

READER 3: How do we show gratitude for this love?
AUDIENCE: By thanking him.
READER 1: Thank Him for our food and for our trials:
READER 2: By resisting a foolish heart.
READER 1: By showing generosity.
READER 2: By rejecting foolish talk.
READER 1: By shunning obscenity.
READER 2: By avoiding coarse jokes.
AUDIENCE: By accepting his victory.

READER 1: In everything make your requests know to God through thanksgiving.
READER 3: He has become our salvation.
AUDIENCE: His love does endures forever.
READER 3 : Let us praise God forever for this enduring love
AUDIENCE: and glory
READER 3: and wisdom
AUDIENCE: and honor
READER 3: and power
AUDIENCE: and strength
READER 3: and salvation.
AUDIENCE: Our God lives!

READER 2: Lord—
AUDIENCE: Lord God Almighty, we give thanks to you,

READER 1: because you have taken
READER 3: your great power
READER 2: and have begun to reign in our hearts.
READER 3: And we give thanks to you
AUDIENCE: for your enduring love.

About the Authors

Melvin Campbell has spent all of his life in academia: teaching chemistry, religion, mathematics, badminton and as of late teaching teachers to teach. His doctorate (Ph.D. Purdue) in chemistry provided him with a unique way of looking at the Biblical stories and how they relate to one's personal life. Campbell has the opportunity of presenting these readings to many audiences in churches and workshops throughout the U.S., Canada, and various places in the world. He makes his home in Riverside, California with his wife. Both are avid bird watchers.

Edwin Zackrison is a trained theologian (Ph.D. Andrews) who has articulated the gospel as a church pastor and a university religion professor. As an accomplished clarinetist he soon saw the value of the arts in communicating the great Biblical themes. Through formal training at a variety of universities Edwin became a prolific producer and director of musical theatre, much of which was based in the moral values of scripture. As the son of printer he brings clarity and precision to these creative writings. A transplanted Californian, he now lives in Ringgold, Georgia with his wife and son.

0-595-29227-5